CARE CROSSES THE RIVER

CARE CROSSES THE RIVER

MERIDIAN

Crossing Aesthetics

Werner Hamacher

Editor

Translated by Paul Fleming

Stanford
University
Press

———————

Stanford
California

CARE CROSSES THE RIVER

Hans Blumenberg

Stanford University Press
Stanford, California

Care Crosses the River was originally published in German in 1987
under the title *Die Sorge geht über den Fluß.* ©Suhrkamp Verlag
Frankfurt am Main, 1987.

The translation of this work was supported by a grant from the
Goethe-Institut, which is funded by the German Ministry of
Foreign Affairs.

Printed and bound by CPI Group (UK) Ltd, Croydon, CR0 4YY

Library of Congress Cataloging-in-Publication Data

Blumenberg, Hans.
  [Sorge geht über den Fluss. English]
  Care crosses the river / Hans Blumenberg ; translated by Paul
Fleming.
      p. cm.--(Meridian, crossing aesthetics)
  "Originally published in German in 1987 under the title Die
Sorge geht über den Fluss."
  ISBN 978-0-8047-3579-7 (cloth : alk. paper)--ISBN 978-0-
8047-3580-3 (pbk. : alk. paper)
  1. Literature--Philosophy. I. Fleming, Paul, 1968- II. Title. III.
Series: Meridian (Stanford, Calif.)
  PT2662.L86S6713 2010
  834'.914--dc22   2010013353

Typeset by Bruce Lundquist in 10.9/13 Adobe Garamond

Contents

MARITIME EMERGENCIES

Cursing the Sea   3

Suffering Shipwreck Professionally   3

Enemies   4

Remaining Inconspicuous   5

A Heretic on Board, on the Adriatic and the Danube   6

The Heightened Casuistry of the Maritime Emergency   9

Shipwrecked and Unable to Swim   12

The Promise of Rescue Taken at Its Word   13

Renouncing Rescue Right on Time   15

Hungry for Figs Again   16

The Deadly Calm of the Sea   24

WHAT IS PERHAPS LOST

Rescue by Sinking   31

Darwin's Ship Bible   32

Gestures of a Loss of Reality   33

The Suspicion of Meaninglessness   39

The Restlessness of the Spirits   43

A Loss of the Last Judgment   44

Aversion to Knowledge   49

Side Effects of the Need for Meaning   53

Remnants of the Unattainable   56

The Last of All Cult Victims: Boredom   60

Names Prescribe Burdens and Losses   61

Rescues Without Sinking   64

FUNDAMENTAL DIFFERENCES

Foundation and Soil, Bottom and Ground:
Hitting Bottom, Getting to the Bottom of Things,
Standing on the Ground   67

Standing and Constancy   70

The Building Site   71

Farmland   74

The Swamp   75

"Asphalt" and "Swamp"—A Dualism   78

Beneath the Foundations   80

Terra Inviolata   82

On Board · Transformations of a Metaphor   85

SOMETHING LIKE A WORLD ORDER

The Secrecy of All-too-easy Formulas   93

Missing Timeliness   94

A Talent for Guilt   94

Visibility   95

Detours 95

King Pyrrhus · Life as a Detour 97

Systematics of Fate 98

A Case of Melancholy 100

Border Post and Gravestone · A Daemon's World Orders 101

Three Degrees Above Nothingness ·
On the Symbolism of Theoretical Insults and Consolations 106

The Arbitration of the World 109

A Proviso for the Beatified ·
Lead-Up to an Auxiliary Thought of Malte Laurids Brigge 110

Unexpected Congruence 113

MISSED ENCOUNTERS

Parable of the Unmissable Missed Encounters 117

In Many Places 118

   On Rhodes 118

   In Rome 119

   In Rome, Somewhat Later 121

   In Vienna 122

   In Frankfurt 123

   In an Alpine Pasture 124

   In Jena 126

   In the East 127

Summit Talks 128

   Hebbel at Schopenhauer's 128

   Proust and Joyce 133

DASEIN'S CARE

The Narcissism of Care:
The Creature of a Fleeting Reflection   139

The Fundamental Concern of Being   141

Concern for a Final Unmistakability   143

Concern for the Worthiness of Being   145

Concern for Reason   148

Taking Care of Happiness   149

If Care Is Objective, Happiness Must Be Subjective   152

Tense World Relations   153

A Still Unconfirmed Last Word   157

CARE CROSSES THE RIVER

CARE CROSSES THE RIVER

Maritime Emergencies

Cursing the Sea

A shipwrecked person thrown on the shore in one of Aesop's fables awakes from the first sleep of exhaustion and finds the sea calm again. Seized with rage, he curses his destroyer: the sea entices people with her beautiful face, he says, only to ruin them when they follow her. In the shape of a woman, Thalassa, the Sea, responds to the wrathful man: *Don't curse me, curse the winds, since by nature I am no different than the earth. The winds, however, descend upon me and churn me into wild waves.*[1]

As is so often the case in fables, the moral of the story seems far removed from what one expects. When injustice occurs—so it is passed down—one should not fixate on those who have acted unjustly if they are dependent on others who have commanded them to do so. Annoying, if that is supposed to be the moral of the story.

The fable is beautiful but not perfect. It disappoints, because the winds get stuck with the fact that the sea can equate itself with the solid earth, and can thus invoke its *physis*, which for the Greeks was the most convincing claim. The fable is a fragment; the winds, likewise reproached by the shipwrecked person, still have to have their say.

Something like this: *The sea is not like the land. When we winds descend upon the land, it doesn't move. For this to happen, the one who causes the earth to quake is necessary. If the sea didn't accommodate us, there would be no waves, no shipwrecks.*

Suffering Shipwreck Professionally

Shipwrecks belong to fates that possess a classical stature. In the lives of the Greek philosophers, shipwrecks appear as mobile testing grounds; following his second letter to the Corinthians, the Apostle Paul suffered three shipwrecks (Acts of the Apostles only grants him one). Goethe came close enough to shipwreck between Messina and Naples, and in the short

---

1. Blumenberg does not cite the sources of his quotations anywhere in the original German text, which lacks both notes and bibliography. The notes, glosses, and other clarifications given in square brackets [ ] are my own.—Trans.

epic poem "Alexis and Dora," he has the hero on board the ship long for it to sink so that dolphins can carry him, a nonswimmer, back to his lover, who has perhaps already betrayed him. The price of reaching safety from gnawing doubt is extreme endangerment.

For philosophers, this is the obligatory path: How else can one teach about ultimate and penultimate things, if one hasn't been exposed to them? Notorious nonswimmers that philosophers have always been, one clung to a plank from the shattered ship, let oneself be washed ashore, and then continued teaching at the nearest academy as if nothing had happened. And that was the point: one was a philosopher to the degree that one was immune to such interruptions. Of course, one had to be sure that the inland was inhabited, proof of which were geometrical figures left in the sand at the appropriate moment and not washed away, as if this had been the main thing done on beaches since the beginning of time. The virtual omnipresence of preconditions was the core element of Platonism. It follows from the theory of anamnesis that the mathematician was at home throughout the world and could get down to work right away after every shipwreck.

And thus it remains up to today. The fates of emigrants prove it. After the age of real shipwrecks come the metaphoric ones: the expelled or fleeing foreigner, still unskilled in the country's language, fills his writing tablets here just as he did back there. Platonism is a philosophy for shipwrecks; it turns them into episodes, while languages turn them into catastrophes, even and especially if one wants to speak of universality, as long as it is only the universally human—in this case, no straight path leads from the saving shore to the schoolhouse full of people waiting to learn. Perhaps this experience above all belongs to the experience of professional survivors of maritime emergencies.

Enemies

Two enemies take to sea on the same ship. In order to be as far as possible from one another, the one proceeds to the bow of the ship, the other to the stern. And there they remain. Suddenly seized by a storm, the ship begins to sink; the one at the stern asks a sailor which end of a ship sinks first. The bow, is the answer. *Then I no longer regret my death as much; it affords me the chance of seeing my enemy drown to death first.*

The story found its way into the corpus of Aesop's Fables and has gotten stuck there. It supposedly complies with the moral at the fable's end: out of hatred of their enemies, many people are willing to endure horrible things as long as they can witness their enemies' misfortune in the process. This morality fits the story poorly, since neither person took ship in order to experience the other's demise. Rather, the other's demise is a small consolation once one's own death appears to be inevitable. Anyhow, the fable is too complicated for the Aesopian milieu. We cannot ask and find out what the other person says and does, when he learns that he will sink first with the bow. Shouldn't he be allowed to think that his enemy's prolonged fear of death at the stern at least compensates for the latter's Schadenfreude?

The Aesopian fable does not know the subjunctive mood, and it certainly does not tolerate psychological sophistication. This story deserved to escape the dead-end of genre typology. The naïveté of the fable requires that the two enemies be capriciously distributed to bow and stern: the one goes there because the other is already standing here. Therefore, only during the maritime emergency is it revealed that this distribution of places and chances offers the opportunity for immorality, which begins with the question of which end sinks first and ends in delight.

A refinement of the fable (one that it doesn't know, and rightfully so) would be to forego the real shipwreck and be content with a potential one. In this case, one of the enemies inquires already before the ship sets sail where one is safest during a maritime emergency (which is still the case with train and airplane travelers today, as everyone has experienced). When he learns that the stern is safest and secures a place for himself there, the other boards the ship, sees the one disinclined to him, and heads to the bow. He perhaps never finds out the disadvantage tied to this position; his enemy at the stern, however, begins to play with the mere possibility of the satisfaction that a rising storm and sinking would afford him. At the end of the trip, he would disembark with the feeling of being favored. For some, this suffices for letting one's enemies live. For morality this doesn't suffice, but it is enough for survival.

Remaining Inconspicuous

Sea travel is risky for philosophers not only because of the shipwrecks that typify the profession. There are also always other difficult situations in which one expects more from philosophers than from others.

Bion of Borysthenes, a Scythian and former slave, who was his master's heir and burned the master's rhetorical writings in accordance with his guild, left behind scarcely more than a few blunt Cynic sayings and anecdotes, one of which Francis Bacon deemed worthy of inclusion in his collection of apophthegma. A restless wanderer between the schools of wisdom as well as between the islands and the cities, Bion was often at sea and more hardened against its threats than many a sailor. This was proven when a storm of such violence fell upon the ship that the wild, godless sailors began to beseech the gods. The philosopher, himself a good atheist with hedonistic traits, commanded the seamen to be quiet; they would only draw the gods' attention to themselves: *Peace, let them not know ye are here.*

The moral: whoever doesn't believe in the gods is better off not praying to them even when in need.

A Heretic on Board,
on the Adriatic and the Danube

Leibniz too was in Italy. Between March 1689 and March 1690, from Venice down to Naples. On May 9, 1689, he even climbed Vesuvius.

Leibniz traveled at the behest of his prince in order to find sources for a history of the House of Welf. The genealogical connection with the House of Este in Ferrara was considered to be a legend. Leibniz—and otherwise he wouldn't be Leibniz—found the proof.

This loftier purpose maybe prevented him from also writing an "Italian Journey." We only know the stories he told, and these through his later assistant J. G. Eckhart.

Scarcely any of the early travelers to Italy could get around a sea trip. At sea, one avoided the bad roads, the lurking robbers, and gazed cheerfully upon the long shores. Until everyone inevitably encountered a sea storm.

Leibniz embarked in Venice, sailing along the coast "in a small ship totally alone." Which means as the only passenger. Then "a horrible storm" arose. Eckhart reports that Leibniz often told him that the sailors—thinking he didn't understand their language—"agreed among themselves and in his presence to throw him overboard and to divide his possessions among themselves." A Leibniz knows how to help himself even here. For every situation, he has the right thing ready. In this case, a rosary, which he pulls out as if it were the time for it. They see him praying. Hereupon, one of the sailors tells his mates that he doesn't have the heart to kill the passenger, since one sees that he is not a heretic. Leibniz thus escaped with his life and disembarked near Mesola.

Leibniz cannot have told the story as it is handed down. The one seaman's bailing out of the plan of robbery-murder is only understandable if the accomplices were not originally intending to rob Leibniz. The dreadful storm must have led them, in their simple faith, to believe that it was their heretical German passenger who had brought the wrath of God down on them, endangering life and limb, and that to assuage the deity, they had to throw this nuisance overboard. The fact that the prospect of ill-gotten gains accompanied this God-fearing aim in no way mollifies the observer's moral disapproval; it only renders understandable why Leibniz's use of the rosary could remove the motive for getting rid of him. It proves that the predatory motivation would not have been enough to cost him his life. The strongest apotropaic object was used against the strongest impulse.

For precisely this reason the story must be examined more carefully. The report, as it is transmitted to us, has Leibniz pretend something in two ways. First, he certainly did not let on (and no one will find this questionable) that he knew the sailors' intention because he understood their language. This would seem a bit improbable, since the language of seamen always tends to be incomprehensible even for the one fluent in the language of the land. Wouldn't it be much more plausible that the traveling foreigner, out of preventive intelligence, prepared himself for the possibility that the superstitious sailors might hold him responsible for the wrath of the elements, just as foreigners at all times have come under suspicion of having given the gods cause for plague or drought? Leibniz didn't understand a word the sailors said—that is a belated rationalization. But he knew how people thought, and thus what he was facing: a German heretic in a storm at sea—where wouldn't he have been viewed as the price for calming the deity? Didn't someone in Venice advise him to take a rosary along for all eventualities, a rosary that the adviser might have believed to possess different powers altogether than that which it then actually performed?

The second element of deception in Leibniz's behavior is more dubious. One should imagine it in the form of a question posed to Kant: is one allowed to act as if one were praying when one isn't praying at all? And in addition, can one do this according to the base rituals of a religion that one doesn't belong to and doesn't believe in just to save one's life? Every

Kantian would be faced with a dilemma, one not caused by any doubt about Kant's imagined answer—about which there can be no doubt—but rather caused by morality's ability to bear this answer, which even a Kantian might only imagine him- or herself capable of. The version that has come down to us explicitly states that Leibniz only "acted as if he were praying." If this is the way he told the story, then this is the way the story must be told about him. But precisely because of the indubitable nature of such narrative constraint, it remains dubious. A horrible storm at sea—even a Leibniz is afraid. In this situation, many a person has prayed who didn't really know how to pray. It isn't a disgrace to think that in the midst of such a storm, Leibniz grasped at the straw that might prayerfully lead him through the labyrinth of his distractions.

Much more important is what the scene elucidates: this ritual, which he wouldn't have performed out of conviction, couldn't have cost Leibniz much effort. On the contrary, one must think of the satisfaction with which he might have repeatedly told this story, because it contains something like the demonstration of his superior confessional pluralism: a tolerant person, who, heeding Epicurus's advice, follows the local custom and sacrifices to the gods of the country. In the history of religions, one finds not only the impressive fact of religious rigor and martyrs but also, as a contrast to this (especially in approaching forms of enlightenment), the impressive act of those who believe they can unite in their person all possible human divisions and fragmentations. They share the leniency of their rational God with the imaginative industriousness of humans soliciting His favor. During the storm at sea, with a rosary in his hand, Leibniz shows that one can even do this without harming spirit and reason.

One last look at the storm-tossed little ship risks exaggeration through a further reversal of motivations. Let us suppose that the sailors had in fact decided to rob the German with all that luggage right from the start. When they had their hands full with maneuvering the ship in the storm and, as far as they were concerned, could do nothing right for their deity, only then did they suddenly see the praying passenger as the guarantee for overcoming the threatening danger and might possibly, in addition, ascribe their salvation to this equally foreign and pious man. It might thus not only have been toleration that overrode their intention to rob him. An aura of inviolability had arisen around the passenger, and upon the wind's abatement, this protected him from being the target of any predatory desires. He disembarks as one who has done his part.

We could leave it at that, if someone who looked at this little piece had not unearthed something so fitting from his inexhaustible, erudite fund as to make a postscript necessary.

Georg Friedrich Meier was not as famous as [Alexander Gottlieb] Baumgarten, the founder of the new global discipline of "aesthetics." Like the latter, however, Kant made him essential as a textbook author for his lectures through Meier's *Auszug aus der Vernunftlehre* (*Excerpt from the Theory of Reason*) (1752). A student of [Christian von] Wolff's, Meier also wrote a *Rettung der Ehre der Vernunft wider die Freygeister* (*Defense of the Honor of Reason Against the Freethinkers*) (1747), which was published in Halle one year before the *Anfangsgründe aller schönen Künste* (*First Principles of All Fine Arts*) and contained a section entitled "On the Freedom to Speak." Without looking much further into causes, this section offered the opportunity to address the casuistry of frankness in religious matters: whether we may pretend to hold the opposite of our true opinion, because, for example, we would otherwise be *robbed of our entire earthly happiness or indeed our life*. At just this juncture, Meier cites Leibniz, who is now traveling on a boat to Vienna on the Danube River; and this time as well he is alone among Italians. The "horrible storm" that is necessary for producing the critical situation rose up, and the sailors immediately recognized the heretic on board to be its cause. When Leibniz in the cabin hears what they have in store for him, he pulls out the rosary—however he may have come by it—and sits down "on a chair with the most devout expression in the world." Those entering the cabin with "murderous intentions" are rendered speechless, and are left with nothing to do but regret their intentions and let the philosopher live. The author casts a glance full of anticipation at the reader and asks "whether Leibniz could have gone about it differently? Whether he could have done the true religion even the smallest service if he had presented himself as a Protestant, if only by merely remaining silent?" No need to wait for the reader's answer. [Meier's] §44 concludes with this question.

The Heightened Casuistry of the Maritime Emergency

Moral casuistry is of interest only to strict moralists; in the extreme cases where life is threatened, moral laxity acquires almost every license, thus sheltering all of morality's fundamental principles from the test of holding water. The *Ius necessitatis* (law of necessity) must be strictly applied so that the conflicts it is supposed to "regulate" can generally be identified by means of thought experiments.

Kant—as almost to be expected—twice mobilized shipwrecked people in order to elucidate what for him is an important distinction in the law of necessity. The lenient principle that necessity knows no law (*necessitas non habet legem*), Kant writes, should not grant a drowning person the right to wrench the saving plank from another so as to secure it for oneself. Rather, this principle, Kant continues, concerns every legislator's objective resignation in not being able to connect a punitive sanction to the law that prohibits saving one's own life by surrendering the life of another (that is, by the absolute mediatization of another's life). And this is the case because the "threat of a still uncertain evil (death by judicial sentence) cannot outweigh the fear of a certain evil (that is, drowning)." Kant considers the legislator, who may not get entangled in the contradiction of using sanctions whose ineffectiveness is as clear as the validity of the precept [*Vorschrift*] against a clearly unjust act. The "act of violent self-preservation" is thereby in no way excusable or, in Kant's vocabulary, "non-culpable" (*inculpabile*); rather, it is consigned to something like impunity, which is therefore called "subjective impunity," although it doesn't consider the shipwrecked person's conflict between self-preservation and the preservation of another, but rather and exclusively the legislator's quandary in the conflict of determining the purpose of his own action. Under these circumstances, primarily the delinquent act and then also the delinquent person are "non-punishable" (*impunibile*). He who survives by culpable means goes unpunished; his guilt remains his business.

But as with every casuistry of extreme cases, the probing question arises as to whether the extent of possible conflict has truly been exhausted, when the mediacy [*Mittelbarkeit*] of punishment (to life) cannot, in fact, be greater than the immediately averted loss (of life). Admittedly, Kant makes it an express condition that the shipwrecked person trying to rescue himself must "be in the same mortal danger as the other person." Still, the initial situation of his violent act is not adequately determined, as one can easily glean from the other citing of the case, where Kant says that the drowning person pushes "another shipwrecked person from his plank." Here the mortal danger is not the same, as would be required by Kant: the one in possession of the floating plank is in any case not yet lost, the one pushing him away would be if he didn't do so. He steals the other person's means of rescue. Here the injustice is graspable, precisely because the two shipwrecked people's initial situation is not equal. The action is too close to the blind reflex of self-preservation, of bare impulsiveness. Casuistry always starts getting difficult when a person must include and has included another person's possible action in his decision. With complete equality of both people's situation—understood as sharing the same plank—the consideration as well as the suspicion, indeed, the probability cannot be excluded that the other could improve his situation and prospects of rescue (and, therefore, would want to improve these) by pushing his partner from their plank. Only now does something enter the picture that tends to get short shrift in all casuistry: preemption [*Prävention*].

Given the part that morality played in the emergence of "anthropology," it is astonishing how rarely this fundamental trait of humanity—that is, not just reacting to what is given and knowable, but rather preemptively confronting the first possible thing—is thematized and integrated into theoretical inquiries into foundational matters. Human beings, in possession of concepts, act in relation to what is absent, what is unperceivable; they "react" to mere suspicion. In this respect, human beings constitute the one mistrustful living being, and persuading them to trust—when it really matters—is mere rhetoric most of the time. Trust is the result of experiences in an always limited range of tolerance, since rarely does experience teach us how to act when it's a matter of life and death. The casuistry of shipwreck is not allowed to make the improbable its guideline, for example, father and son surfacing on one and the same plank. If mutually unknown, the two survivors can be neither indifferent to nor trusting of each other. The liminal situation consists in the fact that only the person who pushes the other from the plank—and thus makes it seaworthy—will survive. As so often, morality would be the hesitation at the presupposition of whether the other person would, for his part, truly resort to the same means. He would as soon as he recognized what might depend upon this push.

Humans are creatures of hesitation because, and as long as, they keep their distance from what provokes their actions. This distance can be one of space or of time. Two shipwrecked people clinging to the same plank that doesn't support both have lost distance. When Kant commands that one observe them without this intensification, Darwin is still far ahead in the future, and hence consideration of the case in the interest of the species: although the person who saves himself only then to die by hanging may have won nothing for himself, he is nevertheless likely to have the most fleeting chance of procreating—as an ancestor of those who decide on the spur of the moment, of those for whom hesitation may become more and more alien, if one considers them again and again in maritime emergencies and similiar situations. Humanity would lose again what its prehistory had won for it, in that it brought humanity the advantage of distance: to let that which is to come, not the present, tip the scale. This, however, did not make humans trusting.

Shipwrecked and Unable to Swim

The poet and dramatist Christian Friedrich Hebbel also had his version of being shipwrecked, which he noted down on May 25, 1837, in Munich, in his self-explanation vis-à-vis his former benefactress Amalie Schoppe.

Were he to drown in the ocean, Hebbel writes, he wouldn't "see in it fate's private hatred of me, as perhaps earlier, but merely the proof that I couldn't swim." At first glance the Epicurean speaks here, one who resists the thought that what strikes him was intended for him. To this end, Epicurus had renewed and further developed the theory of the greatest possible distribution of all the world's coincidences: atomism. Viewed as an absolute metaphor, atomism is the antithesis of Stoicism's notion of providence. No notion of a guiding force behind the world can be content with gratefully accepting the favorable allotments of the way of the world; it also has to prepare for the blows that are still to come. Rather than being grateful for these blows, the Stoic exhibits the steadfastness of one who has already foreseen such misfortune as too small to be worthy of his attention.

The Epicurean doesn't feel that he was the target when he is struck. Hebbel goes a step further than atomism. A person who suffers shipwreck in the metaphoric ocean and sinks has failed to master either the technique of ship construction and navigation—or, now, fails to master the art of swimming. A human being wants to be able to ascribe his own fate to himself, even when fate seizes him with deadly force. If the world didn't hate him even in this situation, perhaps he had only failed to recognize its love.

In 1843, in Hamburg, Hebbel will again draw upon the shipwrecked person for his diary. He poses a dark question to himself: "Does the shipwrecked person love the plank that he so resolutely clings to?" One doesn't need the art of hermeneutics in order to recognize Hebbel's pondering his relation to Elise Lensing. Thanks to Elise's sacrifices, he didn't drown in the ocean of his fate. The fact that a debt of gratitude can block the possibility of love to the point of hatred is not a new piece of wisdom. Hebbel's question goes further: Wouldn't drowning have been preferable to the loss of freedom through this debt? One is not free to choose one's own tragedy: the saving plank strips the shipwrecked person of every choice. For this reason, one already finds a "no" in Hebbel's question. As he sees himself, he is one who was not *allowed* to be rescued.

The Promise of Rescue Taken at Its Word

The notion that you are what you eat appeared to the nineteenth century as one of the great moments of sobering up during the descent from the heights of idealism, which was an object of pride more on account of its audacity than its truth. In a slightly varied form, this notion is a biological triviality: you become what you eat. But the secret that you thereby remain what you were—the enigma of identity in the flux of metabolism—was not even touched upon.

The elementary process of self-preservation described in this sentence—you are what you eat—also contrasts, however, with what one *can* do without *being* it. Ingesting food means that the human must ingest by devouring and destroying in order to be, while being permitted to remain what he is. *It* cannot remain, so that the *human* may remain. This is a process that can only take place in the tightest parameters of reality, the domain of human nutrition. When the human goes too far in satisfying itself on the world without doing something for it in return, the world remains unconcerned with it, indolent against it, revenges itself with desertification.

The fact that the human is a being that *wants* to become what it eats (as opposed to merely accepting this fact as a necessity) is reflected in the species-specific cannibalism that marks most of human history, whose overcoming was one of the greatest restrictions culture imposed on human appetites. As his diary shows, for Hebbel, who never euphemized his cannibalistic hunger for reality, but rather attributed it to the poet's demiurge-like right to barbaric regression, the fable of the wolf and the lamb goes beyond the mere hunger of the predator: "The wolf was told so often that it had nothing of the lamb in it that it finally decided to eat the lamb in order to have all of the lamb."

Swallowing reality whole so as not to lack even a bit of it is arguably the ultimate metaphor for all realism. Therefore, the most audacious expression of religious longing for unity with the deity—and the sole defense against God's capriciousness and superiority—is allowing believers to eat their God. Every anxious recourse to symbolism surrenders the boldness found in this form of assuring salvation.

On the other hand, such access to God's favor via incorporation comes up against the limitations that were definitively imposed on barbarism, or appeared to be. One might object that precisely this one central idea of those hungry for salvation eating their God subsumes all misguided desires, since God's infinity guarantees that those who nourish themselves on Him in no way diminish that most precious of all substances, divinity itself. And yet the opposing tendency toward symbolism, toward merely and piously being content with the sign of grace, remains a cultural defense that must not be expunged from history. This shows itself whenever culture's hungry cry for reality, for a whole and all-inclusive "realism," resounds in areas other than religion, arousing fears that the outcry might be as seriously intended as it appears to be, and not just calculated to shock the petite bourgeoisie.

"Realists" don't like to hear the word "consciousness"—for them it tends too much toward idealistic notions. There is something to this. It concerns, however, not only, or not in the first place, epistemological specialties; it is fundamental to the ability to preserve a culture in the crudest sense. The fact that we can know something, that we are capable of possessing something in consciousness, means nothing less than being able to *have* something without having to *be* it. Consciousness is the organ for not devouring the world and still being able to possess and enjoy it.

We can describe and define this distance to bodily incorporation; we cannot explain it. Because of the remainder of dissatisfaction that such a distance to the "thing [*Sache*]" contains and maintains, we shall never be free of the enticements of realism understood as the totality of conquering and absorbing. The sense that "we want it all!" will never fall silent; this is the threat of humanity, its anthropological antinomy, derived from its own relation to the world.

On December 2, 1985, papers subscribing to the Evangelical Press Ser-

vice news agency reported that four Papua New Guinean fishermen drift-
ing in the Pacific Ocean after a shipwreck survived for six days, "because
they read the Bible and ate it page for page." The now almost extinct
genus "critics of ideology [*Ideologiekritiker*]" would certainly read the
last line of the report with satisfaction: "The German Bible Society in
Stuttgart reported this story over the weekend." Having become a bit less
"critical," one may enjoy to the point of disbelief this piece of realistic
survival-art.

Renouncing Rescue Right on Time

Again and again, people's behavior at sea provides us with the most
profound metaphors for a life whose ground can never be firm enough to
make one forget its relations to nautical risk. "Formerly [*Früher*], many
sailors didn't want to learn to swim," Ernst Jünger notes in his late diaries,
adding by way of explanation that they had "their reasons for this." The
naming of these reasons can apparently be omitted; it would disturb the
profundity.

This double dictum [*Doppelsatz*], however, already contains an explanation for an even more general obscurity: for the premise that pain dwells
in time or, more precisely, *also* in time. The attraction for the reader in
letting two obscure ideas lie side by side consists in bridging the hiatus:
whoever could swim increased the chance of rescue after a shipwreck only
slightly—but in an acknowledged misrelation to the risk of extending the
hopeless battle for a forfeited life. The logical connection between these
two ideas lies in a circumstance that is not immediately apparent: whoever learned to swim cannot want not to swim. The previous decision to
learn to swim implies not being able to forget it in the case of emergency,
as is the case with any *character indelebilis.*

What Jünger doesn't mention is the obsolescence of this situation. Why
need it be said that this was the case "formerly," but no longer so today—
in fact, that the situation has been reversed? Technology has—along with
so many things that have succumbed to it—also destroyed an absolute
metaphor. No reserved space can guarantee its survival—except for the reserved space of memory, imagination, and the mediation of the harmless
little word "formerly," whose mere existence makes everything like former
times in the realm of metaphor.

The chances of the shipwrecked person who could swim were slim until radio distress signals made it possible for the nearest ships to be led to the scene of the accident.

The relationship between time and pain is reversed here as elsewhere. Every extra minute that one could stay afloat increased one's chances of rescue. Such progress called to mind the disregarded natural art of swimming. It annulled the profundity of Jünger's double dictum as practical wisdom; but *memoria* is strong enough to carry along what progress has superseded. Those who despise progress fail to consider the conditions that alone enable them to be understood.

This double dictum is one of the traces of former, heroic nihilism, traces that the aesthetic renunciation of reflection has transformed into erratic blocks. Jünger sympathizes with the nonswimmer's resolve to lend the indeterminable situation the contours of finitude in the case of a shipwreck. The situation can only be absolute if it knows no transitions. This may not be left to the moment.

Hungry for Figs Again

Goethe was a man of life, whose waning he refused to acknowledge in himself. He found it difficult when death struck close to him. Prior to the intimate friendship of their later years, Karl Friedrich Zelter informed Goethe that, unable to see a way out of an unrealizable promise of marriage, his oldest son had shot himself, leaving Schiller's *Don Carlos* open on his desk at the words: "Is there then no salvation? Not even through crime?—There is none!"

What Goethe has to say as consolation is strangely clumsy and evasive. If a person grows weary of life, Goethe writes, one should only feel sorry for him, not scold him. As the author of *Werther*, he knows this, having himself escaped the waves of death back then. And not only back then: Goethe claims to have saved himself from "many later shipwrecks" with difficulty and to have laboriously recuperated. But it is not the sense of "such is life" that forms the consoling connection and universality, which one can gain from this and build upon; rather, Goethe writes, this is the manner in which all those who have been endangered and stranded tell their story, because only those who escape can tell a story. Herein lies the incomparability with the muteness of the one who can no longer divulge the meaning of his deed, a deed whose enigma tortures Zelter as father. Goethe considers the other side by surprisingly turning away from sharing his own existential distress, which cannot offer the desired consolation. He concludes his words about Werther's waves of death and later shipwrecks with sentences that seem almost absent-minded, in any case distracting: "And thus are all the tales of sailors and fishermen. After the nighttime storm, one regains the shore; the soaked person dries himself off; and the next morning, when the splendid sun again steps forth upon the glimmering waves, the sea is once again hungry for figs."

Can Goethe's friend in Berlin have understood this? Without answering this question one can get closer to an answer by looking at the fate of a poem that stands out, if not for other elements, then for its use of the same enigmatic formulation of the sea being hungry for figs. Goethe dated the poem February 4, 1781; it has no title and begins with the line "In the redness of a sunset-sky the heavens and the sea lie still . . ." It is the eternal story of the two brothers or friends that Hesiod first turned into literature: one is the settled-down homebody who industriously multiplies his possessions; the other flees the nest and seeks adventure and quick earnings. Goethe has the one who stays behind gaze upon the one leaving with his colorful, beautiful pennants, before he returns to his fields and his limited sphere full of worries. He ponders the uncertain fate of his friend, who can win it all, just as he can lose it all: "You were warned; you appeared protected, / Now let gain and also loss be yours [Du warst gewarnt; du schienst geborgen, / Nun sei Gewinst und auch Verlust sei dein]." The poem ends like this. It begins with the exact words of the one friend warning the other who is enticed by the wide expanses lying in the redness of the sunset-sky: "Back into the sea that wants figs again [Zurück ins Meer, das wieder Feigen will]."

The history of this poem and its interpretation is straightforward, since Goethe never published it and Max Hecker first made it public in 1938.

Philipp zu Eulenburg-Hertefeld owned the manuscript of the poem and first published it in 1897 in a private edition, following his own transcription. The handwritten poem left nothing to be desired regarding the clarity of the first strophe's last line. The editor, however, could not get himself to believe that what was before his eyes made sense. He therefore took refuge in a consistent marine conjecture: "Back into the sea that wants to rise again [Zurück ins Meer, das wieder *steigen* will]." This conjecture could be accepted for the one line, but it did nothing for the poem, for the urgency of the friend's warning.

Max Hecker was able to admit what was in the poem and what he read, because he made a discovery in the annals of erudition. Not only was there a source for the sea being hungry for figs, but even one for Goethe. Hecker surmises that Andreas Schott's *Adagia et Proverbia*, a collection of adages and proverbs published in Amsterdam in 1612, could have provided Goethe with this striking turn of phrase. The only proof, however, that can be mobilized to support this assumption is an entry in Goethe's diary from May 21, 1797—much too late for a poem originating in 1781. The lack of earlier evidence for knowledge of the collection naturally does not exclude it.

What Hecker doesn't see, however, must have priority. In the clearest of words, Goethe reveals his familiarity with another, more significant source, one that belonged to his library: on December 16, 1797, he recommends to Schiller that he "get a copy of Erasmus's *Adagia*, which is easy to find." Although this piece of evidence, too, comes considerably later than the poem, it indicates a constant and long-term use of the anthology put together by the Rotterdam humanist Erasmus. Goethe held such collections of sayings in high regard and was proficient in formulating his own sayings and reformulating old ones. In Erasmus, he could see the extent to which this saying was to be found in almost all of the extant proverb-collections from antiquity.

Under the heading *Siculus mare*, this saying is the point of the story of a Sicilian who, on a risky voyage for profit, suffered shipwreck with a load of figs; sometime thereafter, he is sitting on the beach, gazes at the calm and peaceful sea in front of him, and senses the lure of new ventures. However, he has become immune to the temptation of the all-or-nothing of adventure and expresses this with the words: "I know what you want—you want figs! (Oid' ho theleis, syka theleis)." The way Erasmus distills the moral of the tale, it should apply to all who play with the thought of exposing themselves to danger a second time and contrary to their own experience.

Only many years after the lyrical use of this topos would Goethe himself have the firsthand experience whose metaphorical use was so suggestive to him. It truly becomes what he calls a tale of sailors and fishermen: identifying with Odysseus in the Sirens episode. On the return trip from Messina to Naples in May 1787, Goethe's ship was becalmed in a windless sea (rather than meeting with a violent storm, as many claim). To run aground on the Sirens' cliffs behind Capri would not have been all that bad a fate. But as Goethe wrote at the end of May 1787 from Naples to Duke Carl August in Weimar, he "almost perished in the strangest way:

under a completely clear sky and in a totally calm sea—near death via sea calm . . . ." This experience soon came to fruition in poetry. For the sailor, the peaceful, windless sea is worrisome, a "deadly, dreadful calm." The poem "Safe Journey" forms the counterpart to the poem "Calm Seas": The return of the winds loosens the "anxious bonds," because Aeolus himself enlivens what has become petrified.

Looking from this perspective at the letter of condolence Goethe wrote Zelter a quarter of a century later, one can explain the strange digression without difficulty. The expression that can only be understood in the context of the Sicilian story must have become so familiar to Goethe in the meantime that he uses it harmlessly and thoughtlessly to an addressee who had not enjoyed a classical education, but had instead learned masonry and devoted his life to music. Goethe must have known that Zelter would not be able to make sense of this formulation.

But it is not sufficient to present this contrast of the friends' educational backgrounds as an instance of careless thoughtlessness. Knowing better than most how strong the effect could be of something not understood but felt to be significant, Goethe included the inconsolable father's inability to understand in the calculation. Zelter wouldn't comprehend, but through the resistance offered by what he didn't comprehend, he would start pondering, get distracted, be brought from the father's enigma to another enigma. What has not been understood is humanity's greatest source of consolation. Goethe knew all about this.

Nothing in Goethe's only recently elucidated poem indicates that the separation of the two friends destined for such different paths in life took place in Sicily, whose inhabitants were considered to be especially adventurous and susceptible to risks at sea. Erasmus has the person who in disappointment rejects the greedy sea appear on the scene as a salesman who has already lost his shipment of figs and no longer needs the warnings of a friend. Goethe considers the much earlier, fateful moment of the *first* decision and the separation of the friends. There must have been other people who had already lost their shipments to the sea's appetite for figs and were mentioned in the friend's warning images. The scene of lyrical melancholy demands that fate and separation had just been decided, while Erasmus already has the frivolity of a possible repetition in mind.

The background that has to be assumed for Goethe consists in the originary and primeval nature of the separation of paths in life understood as an archaic conflict; this is represented in Hesiod's *Works and*

Days, where shipwreck still reveals how the gods disapprove transgressing the line set for humanity between land and sea. This corresponds very closely to a fable about a shepherd that the editor Carl Halm included in the Aesopian corpus. By chance a shepherd approaches the coast with his flock and gazes spellbound upon the calm sea lying before him; the desire for sea travel comes over him, he sells his sheep and invests the proceeds in a ship's cargo of dates, with which he sails away and immediately sinks in a storm. After he has lost everything and finds refuge on land only with the greatest difficulty, he sees the sea lying calmly before him again a few days later. Only after someone passes by and praises the calmness of the sea is the shepherd moved to a dismissive response: "It longs again for dates (*phoinikon epithymei*)."

One shouldn't overestimate the difference between figs and dates. As a heading for the proverbial use, Goethe finds the word "figs" in Erasmus and Schott. But what cannot be found in any of the sources that come into consideration for Goethe and, thus, what constitutes the actual innovation of his poem from 1781 is the introduction of the saying into the melancholic moment of friends taking leave, of friends taking different roads toward irreconcilable fundamental forms of being.

One shouldn't forget that the poem, through its gesture toward Hesiod's *Works and Days*, also contains Goethe's situation in Weimar, the turning away from the wide world in favor of the concerns and business upon the fields of a small sphere: renouncing the lure of adventure. The flight to Italy will not change this. With respect to the decade that begins here, the trip to Italy will remain only an episode, no matter how enduring its effects. Goethe had at least taken a vacation from the duke.

After Goethe, in the letter of condolence to Zelter, has returned to the old, familiar formulation, a word appears that could be taken from the moral of the Aesopian version of the story, where one reads that the passions (*pathemata*) often become lessons (*mathemata*) for one who is ready to learn. Goethe seems to take recourse to this when he connects the death of Zelter's son with the state of youth in this year of a new movement. One shouldn't wonder, Goethe writes, about the misdeeds people inflict upon themselves and others. Goethe knows from his experience with his own son how youth is overwhelmed by what it expects from itself and by the ways "it is pushed and pulled by the gigantic surroundings." Since his encounter with Napoleon four years earlier, the rift with the generation pushing for liberation and liberty had been decided for

Goethe, as had the conflict with his own son. This decision was what could have caused him to renew the work of his early years of storm and stress: "I trusted myself to write a new *Werther*, one that would make the people's hair stand on end even more than the first one."

Goethe not only reduced Aesop's pastoral scene to Erasmus's formula; above all, he turned the shepherd's saying into the expression of resignation in the face of repeating the same thing: nothing is learned from experience, nothing from history, just as nothing was learned from *Werther*. Every new day, every up-and-coming generation faces the same lure of faraway lands and adventure, profit and pleasure, for which the sea's hunger for figs stands in as a metaphor. The calmness of the sea assumes physiognomic qualities, without receiving mythical form and name. The Aesopian sea is silent, and this "expresses" its waiting for human foolishness, its lurking and voracious will. Only the shepherd addresses it, and his saying "I know what you want" contains the story's finality: a turning away from risk, a return to dry land, a profiting from what one has learned. This is lost in Goethe's condolence letter to Zelter; the fact that their fathers have already met shipwreck does the sons no good—the sea knows no traces of what once was.

Even if we lack an identifiable background image, Goethe's early familiarity with the saying is proven in his letter to Sophie La Roche of November 20, 1774—that is, dating from the same time as the ode "Prometheus" and high-spirited ice-skating in the fields along the Nidda River. Here he describes his unrest, his desire for distant lands: "A time may come, when I return home. 'The sea demands figs!' I still say now and go on my way [*lasse mich davon*]." Here there is none of the irony of Aesop's shepherd, who withholds every further tribute to the sea since it has already received one. Rather, the originally melancholic saying becomes the acceptance of the risk that comes with fleeing the nest—and precisely this element returns in the consolatory letter to Zelter, only with the negative omen of the sheer unavoidability of youthful foolishness.

It is essential for the graphic power of the ancient anecdote about the sea's voraciousness and humanity's thirst for adventure that the sea doesn't appear in its rage of causing shipwrecks, but rather in the *galēnē* of which the Greeks speak: its glistening calm. Unlike other figures in the fable, the sea doesn't need to show or say anything deceptive and seducing; its hypocritical magnificence suffices. For this reason, one version of the ancient fable introduces a third person who meets the pondering shepherd on the shore and confirms the marvelous view of the sea; the failed sailor does not then address the sea, but responds to the stranger with words that he can just as little have understood as Goethe's friend Zelter: "It wants dates." Since the dialogue concludes here and the fable has found its moral, one may wonder how the stranger might have interpreted the saying; the first possibility that comes to mind is that he saw the shepherd as worshipping his deity, who wanted to have his cult organized around the gift of sweet fruits: the sea must be appeased, and to this end, it demands this harmless sacrifice. This consideration has its deeper sense in the attempt to turn the stranger's lack of knowledge of the shepherd's memory and the latter's mistrust of the sea's calm into a *mythical* misunderstanding. It is not for the main figure of the fable that the sea assumes mythical form and addressability, but rather for the stranger who has been introduced for the sake of dialogue and who provokes this remark, precisely so that it doesn't have to be directed at the sea. By avoiding all mythic-allegorical distortion of the story, this version lets the second person and its attendant mocking severity fall away. The shepherd explains to the stranger that there is a clear reason for the sea's calmness, a requirement of preservation, as the stranger must understand since he is not initiated into the intimacy of enmity that is being played out here in confrontation.

The power concentrated in the image of sweet fruit—dates or figs—that still remains tangible in the mere adage, in the *adagium*, can be observed at a pinnacle of the fable's reception by the fact that it is surrendered in favor of obvious comprehensibility. In the fourth book of his fables in verse, La Fontaine includes "The Shepherd and the Sea [Le berger et la mer]," a version that modifies the center of the shepherd's rejection of the sea. The shepherd obtains his right to address someone through the introduction of water nymphs ("Mesdames les Eaux"), to whom the shepherd refuses what he suspects them of demanding from him, his money: "'You want money, O water nymphs,' / He said, 'Address yourselves, I implore, to someone else . . .' [*Vous voulez de l'argent, ô Mesdames les Eaux, / Dit-il, adressez-vous, je vous prie, à quelque autre . . .*]." Everything the ancient fable refrains from is blithely introduced: personification; abstraction of the disputed amount; transformation of the stranger into another, to whom the allegorical beings should and can turn, because he has no knowledge of them. Everything rushes toward the moral, whose pallor completely dispels the image of one

sitting and pondering on the shore, an image that has not even been developed. La Fontaine not only produced one of his weakest adaptations
of Aesop, but also made visible the extent to which the moral of the
fable—instead of being appended rather abruptly to the fable's image,
as so often in Aesop's tradition—assails the imagination when didactic
over-clarity favors allegory. This decline becomes instructive when one
compares the fable with the reduction to the mere adage in both of
Goethe's letters: by maintaining the central pictorial element, the adage
conserves a remainder of the significance that must have escaped the
first, private editor of the poem, Philipp von Eulenburg, when he didn't
accept the obvious reading of the manuscript and replaced it with a
naturalism that seemed more vivid to him.

It is now also clear what truly constitutes the weakness of Goethe's poem
of February 4, 1781. Goethe divided between two friends what Aesop's
shepherd represented in one person, what constituted in him the phases of
one life story: the temptation he fell prey to and the resistance against any
further temptation, a resistance that grew out of this experience. With the
two friends taking separate paths in life, Goethe has his potential speakers,
while the fable either leads the shepherd to a monologic proclamation to
the sea or must lead a stranger to him, who then prompts the shepherd's
remark. The content of this remark—the citation of figs or dates—derives
its entire meaning, however, from the memory of the one person who suffered shipwreck with a cargo of these fruits and therefore alone knew what
the sea desired. The friend who returns to his fields pronounces something
that in the context of the poem remains incomprehensible—unless one is
among those whose education has included Aesop's fables: "Back into the
sea that wants figs again." Something precedes this, something that is recalled with the "back" and the "again," something probably also related
to sea travel, since this "back" occurs after a return that isn't far back in
the past, all of which could possibly be contained in the line "From your
scarcely reachable hills" preceding the "back." But would this be understandable only to those who know the story of shipwreck as the explana-
tory context for wanting figs?

The strength of the ancient anecdote consists in the mutual identity of
the role-bearers: on one side, the shepherd who presses his bitter experience of escaping country life and shipwreck into one scornful formulation—on the other, the sea that between storm and stillness, threat and
allure, is also one and the same, the sea that has devoured and developed

an appetite for figs. This self-sameness in the confrontation—all the way though the alternation of conditions and forms of life—lends the tension of a great fatefulness to the scene that one is to imagine of the shepherd on the seashore.

The Deadly Calm of the Sea

> As is known, he loved the sea, even if only from the shore.
>
> Golo Mann

In Germany in the summer of 1919, after the loss of the First World War, one had to recuperate within the country's borders, particularly where there was no food shortage. The Berlin publisher S. Fischer and his family went for a few weeks to Glücksburg on the Flensburg Fjord in Schleswig-Holstein, and, following a long-established habit, he tried to bring together a few of his publishing house's regular authors at the Strand Hotel. The effort was only moderately successful. The allure of food seems not to have sufficed for his demanding authors. Thomas Mann, however, came. One had especially suffered in Munich.

Mann writes to his friend Ernst Bertram: "I am Fischer's guest here— he improves the otherwise simple nourishment with strawberries in milk and rum grog." North German scrambled eggs with home fries glistening with butter enraptured him: "It's like being in a heavenly paradise," Mann writes to his daughter Erika.

On one of these days, however, the precious author caused worry for a different reason. The publisher's wife, Hedwig Fischer, remembers that Thomas Mann took her fourteen year-old daughter out into the Baltic in a heavy fisherman's boat and was surprised by a calm. The wide boat was too ponderous to row, and the combined power of both too little. The boat remained at sea well beyond its expected return. The publisher and father—no less concerned in the one role than the other—anxiously paced up and down the beach. "When the boat finally appeared, the returnees were celebrated as if they had escaped mortal danger . . ."

The novelist had grown up next to this sea; the danger could not have frightened him that much. And he was not invested in great comparisons with literary heroes whom nature had distinguished, whether by maritime adventure or in some other way.

Otherwise he would have thought of the strange similarity with a fellow writer who had been cast into mortal danger and fright not by a storm but rather through its opposite: a fatal lack of wind. Just such a calm had fatally delivered this writer's boat to the treacherous currents along the rocky coast off Naples. Goethe, by this time, had acquired a taste for the contrast with the baroque dramatics of the storm; he did so precisely at this point in time and as part of his extensive effort to purge himself of these last traces of having belonged to the youth movement that would be called "Sturm und Drang [Storm and Stress]."

Thomas Mann had also—right at the end of the world-shaking event to which his lengthy exertions were devoted—just put behind him a romantic agitation titled *Betrachtungen eines Unpolitischen* [*Reflections of a Nonpolitical Man*]. Absurdly enough, this didn't see the light of day until October 1918, the last full month of the war, and thus simultaneously confuted its own aim. Before he resumed work on *The Magic Mountain*, which had long been interrupted, Mann had delayed it again by writing an interlude, the highly bourgeois-familiar epic *Gesang vom Kindchen* [*Song of the Little Child*]. The lack of wind in Glücksburg, survived like a mortal danger, was an analogical occurrence in a world where one professionally looked for analogies [*Gleichnisse*].

A lack of wind had once been a metaphor for subduing and settling the passions and, thus, a metaphor for the ideal of a life calmed by reason. The Stoic could live and wanted to live with the sea's calm. It was the Age of Reason, of the Enlightenment that, against the Stoic's ideal, discovered that one lacks the driving energy that first converts the brightness of reason into the dynamics of public effect, of historical impulse, of the capacity to act. A powerful wind had to blow in the sails, if the ship was to be able to hold its direction toward a goal that lies in the infinite distance but nevertheless is determinable. The correction of the metaphor expresses the animosity between reason and idyll, the oddity of the inclination to retreat and cultivate one's garden, which Voltaire's programmatic novel *Candide* had emphasized.

Nothing indicates that Thomas Mann would have discovered a reference or a possibility of reference in his little adventure at sea by Glücksburg: something like a form of mythical repetition, which at the time didn't interest him at all, especially in determining one's way of life and attitude toward the world.

In the comparable situation of windless weather in the gulf of Naples, Goethe was animated and sustained by the mythical relation that he had discovered in Sicily through his great conception of a "Nausikaa" and his fundamentally changed perception of the Odyssean sphere. Thus, as a sea traveler, Goethe was not one who was forced to return to the mainland from Sicily via the sea, after he had left the continent to reach the southernmost point of his journey. He *was* Odysseus. This, taken literally, is the core of the inner intensity of his intention to write a "Nausikaa," which should have been a tragedy, since nothing would remain for her in the fifth act other than "to seek out death." Not one line of all this was written, and later there was only "the fleeting memory." But the "dramatic concentration of the Odyssey" that was realized in his head and dreams transformed what could be experienced in reality. What was particularly transformed was the flight from the volcanically devastated Messina after the "invitation of the Cyclops," the invitation of the demonized governor of the island, whom Goethe could believe he had escaped, because on the way to his palatial cave, he had already followed the servant "calling Odysseus his patron and requesting him to intervene on my behalf with Pallas Athena." The escape from Polyphemus was not, however, release from danger, since Poseidon remained ill-disposed toward this Odysseus, even or precisely when the god ordered the sea to be calm. Looking back at the flight that almost failed, the just abandoned island darkened into a condensed image of the volcanic: "Actually, we had seen nothing but utterly vain attempts of the human race to preserve itself against nature's violence, against the malicious scheming of time, and against the rancor of its own hostile divisions." Goethe also became Odysseus by grasping the meaning of "homecoming" at the turning point of his turning away from Weimar: homecoming is the flight from flight. Only mythical identification, the ritual of repetition, grants so much "significance."

During this part of his journey, Goethe developed a procedural model of self-conception that Thomas Mann would only come to after the completion of *The Magic Mountain* and, thus, a decade after the episode in Glücksburg. It was no accident that this procedural model tends to a mythical prototype that lies not in the distant past of Homer but in the proximity of the Weimar Olympian.

When he experienced the total lack of wind in the Flensburg Fjord, Thomas Mann was already a few years older than the Goethe who had had to deal with the same situation off Naples. Identification is not conditioned by being approximately the same age. At the time of Glücksburg, Goethe's placeholder in literary Germany was Gerhart Hauptmann, an innovator, whose dramatic work had scarcely produced the expectation of ever showing such ambitions. Only after Hauptmann excluded himself from the circle of serious aspirants to Mount Olympus by his foolish fraternization did Thomas Mann discover that this role also suited him. There was no thought of this yet in the Glücksburg days.

We now have to take a regrettable step closer to the truth. When Peter de Mendelssohn published the history of the publishing house S. Fischer in 1970, he had at his disposal the posthumous fragments of the unedited memories of Frau Hedwig Fischer from the archive of her son-in-law and daughter in Camaiore, Tuscany; at the time, Mendelssohn could not know that nine years later, he himself would publish Thomas Mann's extant diaries from the years 1918-21. The novelist's unbridled enthusiasm for the days shared with the publisher's family in Glücksburg are fully laid out here for the first time, including the difficulties that plagued his stomach from so many unusual things among the "amazing food," if only from the red fruit pudding topped with yellow cream. For the date July 27, 1919, one reads with amazement that Frau Fischer went along for the trip in the ponderous fisherman's boat; favoring the dramatization of the failure to return and the homecoming, she kept quiet about the fact that she saw everything from the perspective of those missing and expected back home and could only later have been told about the restlessness and worry on the beach. Thomas Mann discounted the whole thing with two sentences: "Brisk journey. Then the winds turned and slackness ensued, so that the return home was severely delayed and we had to be pulled in with the rowboat."

This is not, of course, all that the diaries bring to light. We learn that the mythical formula of repetition already unexpectedly exercised its dominion over the Glücksburg days. The sentence "It is a shame that I have already written *Tonio Kröger . . .*" in the letter to Ernst Bertram gains in significance when one learns that Thomas Mann had already been in Glücksburg and in this same hotel as a child; that the innkeeper is revealed to be the same Herr Satz; and that the black-eyed companion "Hanni" from back then is also there: "All of this is strange. On top of it the air, the smells, the colors, the language, the type of people. Tonio Kröger, Tonio Kröger. It is always the same and the feelings deep. . . ." Here one finds what one is looking for. As a reaction to the unexpected, the line "all of this is strange" could belong to the typology of Goethe's language.

"Heightened repetition" is not only a formula for a literary style. Before this, it has to be viewed as the structure of being able to experience. Only then can one comprehend how an idyll experienced by an approximately nine-year-old child in Glücksburg thrusts itself in before a school friendship in Lübeck and a painters' friendship in Munich in order to make *Tonio Kröger* possible.

What Is Perhaps Lost

Rescue by Sinking

Among the great fund of emblems, the Stoic byword "Pereant ne peream [May they perish, so that I shall not perish]" is illustrated by the crew of a little ship, lost among towering waves, throwing overboard cargo and possessions—ballast, the surrender of which they hope will save them from ruin.

One seems to be witnessing a ritual: sacrifices to an angry God in order to calm the storm. Humans surrender what had been valuable in order to risk their lives on long journeys. Sacrifices are not to be made in a petty way. "Let it all sink as long as I get away!"

Stoics differentiated between what is proper to oneself and what is foreign, between what is inalienable and what is dispensable, between what can be affected and what is unreachable. From this perspective, property was foreign; one could cast it away without doing any harm to the core of what is proper to oneself. One could be affected, could win and lose with respect to what is foreign to oneself, not with respect to what is proper. Whatever can be cast away, let it perish, so that one cannot be destroyed by associating it too much with what is proper to oneself. Making oneself lighter has to remain a light task; it has to be easy, as Goethe would say, to keep one's little ship afloat on the "wave of the world."

How far can one go with this ritual? The gods are insatiable; they drive up the price of rescue and favor. The gods never hesitated in demanding an Iphigenia in order to produce a little wind. If one looks at the emblem—for example, as it is found on the ceiling of the cloister at Wettenhausen Abbey in Bavaria—the very next moment might be when the ambiguity of the *pereant* links up with the first moment, when it is no longer things and ballast, no longer freight and cargo, but rather one of the sailors: the one the others in their fear could most easily agree upon. Almost unawares, the stoic notion of being independent of things and circumstances would receive its evil deeper meaning, wafting over from cultic ritual.

Simple images of this sort turn us into spectators. They remind us of the proem to the second book of Lucretius's *De rerum natura* [*On the Nature of Things*], in which he has a spectator standing safely on shore observing a ship caught in a raging sea go down with all hands—he watches with neither scorn nor Schadenfreude, and yet for the first time he pleasurably experiences the solid ground beneath him. Lucretius, whose morality has been questioned and who has been taken to task for aesthetic carelessness, is certainly not thinking here of "Pereant ne peream." There is no connection between the sinking ship out there and the safety here, other than the heartfelt weighing of forms of life [*Lebensformen*].

This spectator will not make a sacrifice to the sea god.

Darwin's Ship Bible

In Charles Darwin's ship Bible aboard the *Beagle*, on which he traveled the world from 1831 to 1836, one finds an entry with the date of Creation: October 23, 4004 B.C., 9 A.M.

This is not a document from the distant past. Now, however, it is impossible to have a sense of what the date's beautiful exactness could have meant. After all, 5,835 years was not a comfortable expanse of time that one could "gaze across" from one's own life experience. Even with this exact date, it was "a long time ago" that the world arose. The billions of years that have been added since then and continually increase have excited none of the wonder that was once regarded as the origin of philosophical contemplation. It still is and will continue to be "a long time ago."

With these thoughts, one still hasn't done justice to the entry in the Bible of the man who would later so greatly enlarge biological time. It is the precision of the stated time that is astounding. The chronologists of the Bible—the most famous among them and the one who also changed the world theoretically being Isaac Newton—invested a lot of work and heated discussion in order to create confidence in the noted date. It has the aura of reliability: one doesn't write such things in a Bible if one isn't sure of the matter. And it is "the matter" to which such attention was paid. The Creator was neither emphasized as the contact person for questions of trustworthiness and covenant-loyalty for several or, at least, two pacts in this expanse of time; nor was the quality of His work implied even on this side of the age of "theodicy." It was the correct date and time that mattered.

With this emphasis on correctness, the archaic-sounding entry begins to approach the viewpoint of both the century and the Bible's owner: the "virtue" of exactness is implied, clothed in the transformation of an element of faith's first articles into an enduring piece of intellectual inventory that has assumed the "shape of knowledge."

Suddenly one begins to see how destructive the piously noted date was for the many pages it preceded: a stupendous success as a turning point toward a conclusive loss—also and not least of all through the one who boarded the ship with this holy book.

Gestures of a Loss of Reality

Philosophers have readers and listeners. They are not seen by their readers. Moreover, the products the readers have in their hands are final versions, in which everything that could be taken as a capricious trace of subjectivity is deleted. Listeners, to be sure, perceive the strange and odd aspects of the speaker in front of them, but are guided by the expectation that what is important for them will be something audible—which causes many listeners not even to look up, so as to take notes in peace. In recalling the main points of a lecture, others may remember how a particular, characteristic gesture accompanied what was said and almost unnoticeably marked the secret wish to communicate something not yet expressed, communicating perhaps the last will to express it at all. This memory does duty for what Nietzsche claimed to be able to do even as a reader: that he "read no words without seeing gestures."

Remembering a life philosopher lecturing promises to reveal some of the effort that goes into the very idea of a philosophy that tends thus toward the whole. Ludwig Marcuse recalled two unforgettable gestures of his teacher Georg Simmel, gestures that should be imagined in relation to each other. The first gesture is "how he, bobbing up and down on the exposed side of the lectern, drilled the sharpened pencil into the air—into an invisible material, as it were." Marcuse immediately adds his interpretation: This is to be understood as the gesture of the passionate analytical thinker. After the first came a second gesture that, although more essential, was less noticed: "He left the exposed edge of the lectern; the outstretched pencil sank between his fingers; and with his head lowered he silently crossed back to the other side of the lectern—until he got a grip on himself and was able to continue the lecture." Marcuse's memory even offers advice on how to understand Simmel's turning away from the gesture of poking through what offers no resistance: "In the silent second of forgetting himself, he inwardly annulled what he had just investigated by drilling . . . ." Simmel's many readers all recognize this turning point in so many of his arguments, when he goes beyond the supposedly last attainable formulation, observes the result he just produced from the counter-pole of possibilities, and relativizes it. It was the same in the live performance of the teacher: he left behind what had just been seen but could only silently promise how to go beyond it.

The scene presents itself to memory as a moment of extreme helplessness: as the palpableness of an "immeasurable tragedy" of philosophical thinking, and not only in a contemporary thinker and his thought. He appears to be condemned "to fall into his own arms" in order to prevent himself from exhausting his own logical consistency. Simmel's thought process seemed to be able to become optically perceptible: one saw his pleasure in analysis even in the thin air of the most subtle reality or of what is no longer reality, a reality that could therefore be cruelly and inconsiderately yanked back to the ground of empirical facts. Therefore, before he became a *"Lebensphilosoph* [life philosopher]," Simmel had tested himself with the philosophy of a topic that offers some of the greatest resistance to thought: the philosophy of money.

When Ludwig Marcuse made his observations about Simmel's teaching gesture, Simmel had already philosophically found "life" and inserted it as the placeholder for metaphysics; Husserl, on the other hand, had not yet—and not for a long time to come—made the "life-world" the theme of phenomenology. His students in Göttingen considered him a realist and placed all their expectations in the promised return "to the things themselves." The confusion was consequently great when the master of the phenomenological school published his agenda for a transcendental idealism in 1913 in his book *Ideen* [*Ideas*]. Helmuth Plessner, whose life's work is now spread out before us, reports from this period his observation of Husserl's wish-gesture.

Plessner had presented Husserl with a treatise on Fichte's *Wissenschafts-lehre* [*Science of Knowledge*] so that Husserl's comments could help him clarify how his new conception of consciousness's power differs from Fichte's concept of the creative I. One day on the way home from seminar, Husserl admitted in front of his garden door that all German idealism had always been repugnant to him. His whole life he had searched for reality: "And while he said this he drew forth his thin walking stick with its silver handle and braced it, bent, against the doorpost." For Plessner, this gesture underscoring a lifelong search for reality appears to be the

fundamental figure of phenomenology become incarnate: "In an unsur-
passably vivid manner, the walking stick represented the intentional act,
and the post represented its fulfillment." Thus did Plessner express it in
1959 at the celebration of Husserl's one-hundredth birthday in Göttingen.
Admittedly, the stick as an instrument of contact with reality (an instrument that has become foreign to us today) already belonged to Wilhelm
Dilthey; and Max Scheler referred to it in 1926 when he demonstrated the
opposition of idealism and realism through the experience of resistance—
with the refinement that "when we brace a stick against the wall, the
resistance is experienced at the stick's end, the sense of touch, however,
in the hand. . . ." In his 1890 treatise *Beiträge zur Lösung der Frage vom
Ursprung unseres Glaubens an die Realität der Außenwelt und seinem Recht*
[Contributions to the Solution of the Question of the Origin of Our
Belief in the Reality of the Outside World and Our Right to This Belief],
Dilthey, however, still spoke (as is more appropriate for science) of a probe
[*Sonde*], of how one would scarcely brace it against a wall. Since Scheler
also had contact with phenomenology in Göttingen, one can assume that
the tidings of Husserl's use of the walking stick could have influenced this
distortion of the quotation from Dilthey.

A note in Wittgenstein's *Philosophical Investigations* indicates how natural it is to think of a "probe" as soon as the use of the stick has taken into
account a displacement of the sense of touch: "If I feel this object all over
with a stick, I have the sense of touch in the tip of the stick, not in the
hand that holds it." Like the phantom pain of an amputee, this is in no
way a strengthening of reality consciousness; on the contrary, one suspects
projection at work. Feeling takes place not here but "there":

> "I feel the hardness etc. in the stick's tip." It is thus fitting that while touch-
> ing an object all over with the stick I don't look at my hand but at the end of
> stick, that I describe what I feel with the words "I feel something hard, round
> there" and not with the words "I feel pressure on the fingertips of my thumb,
> index, and middle finger . . ." If someone were to ask me "What do you feel
> in the fingers holding the probe?" I would answer him thus: "I don't know—I
> feel something hard, rough there."

Wittgenstein's undivided concentration belongs to the phenomenon that
I, as someone absolutely coupled with the here-and-now, can nevertheless
qualify something with the sense of touch as a now-and-there. The classical suspicion of modernity doesn't interest him.

Wittgenstein describes—this spares him great doubts. With respect to
the whole, description is also the "solution" of phenomenology, Husserl's
self-emancipation from getting entangled in the obsolete epistemology
that faded with Neo-Kantianism. The postulate of description, however,
only displaces the weakening of reality consciousness onto the refinement
of intuition [*Anschauung*], which again and again has to make sure of
having intuited. A decade after Plessner's memory from Göttingen, Hans-
Georg Gadamer recalled Husserl's teaching gesture from the Freiburg
years. During his lecture, Gadamer reports, Husserl often looked at his
hands, which were completely occupied with having "the right hand's
fingers" circle "in a slowly rotating motion on the rounded palm of his
left hand." Gadamer interprets this gesture as a method of concentration.
This interpretation did not, however, satisfy his hermeneutic vigilance,
since he immediately expands it by adding that "at the same time" this
gesture made "'tangible [*handgreiflich*]' something of the technical [*hand-
werklich*] ideal of precision in Husserl's art of description."

The eyewitness has primacy regarding authentic transmission. Yet looking back over more than half a century, the helplessness of such metaphoric "tangibility" becomes evident. The unfulfillable need to refine the
means of describing the "essential" becomes an indication of the fleeting manner in which what is essential withdraws from the viewer and
compels the gesture of restless industriousness—an industriousness that
is simultaneously fear of not being able to achieve the "infinite work" the
essential demands. This threat of a loss of reality is supposed to be countered in the priority given to the themes of experiencing the other and
intersubjectivity. But we know how little this satisfied those who, at the
end of Husserl's teaching duties in Freiburg, defected to the entirely different "tangibility" of Heidegger's analysis of Dasein, to the proclamation
that cuts through the Gordian knot of the problem of reality: there is no
hiatus between subject and object, the hiatus is the artificial product of a
loss of reality that Dasein experienced through its failure to recognize its
irreversible being-in-the-world.

If one looks back at Husserl's walking stick in Göttingen—which had
to be of contemporary elegance and, thus, of pliable thinness—then
it must have appeared to the observer more as an arc of intentionality
in which phenomenology had recognized consciousness's encompassing
achievement than as an instrument for testing the solidity of the robust
doorpost that resisted it. In contrast, the circling of one hand on the

palm of the other possesses something of the phenomenologist's repeatedly failed attempts to appoint one's own body as the eminent organ of the consciousness of reality. The gesture between hand and hand demonstrates the circular conclusion within the system of one's own body: even the oldest and most invulnerable sense of reality—touch—obtains a dubious satisfaction without having crossed the limit of its immanence.

One finds a parallel to Husserl's hand-in-hand circlings, a parallel without a hint of despair, once again in Wittgenstein. Among the countless fictional scenarios that he plays out, there is one in which the right hand pays money to the left. Then come the questions: Can the right hand give the left hand money as a present? What would this depend on? The right hand could issue a certificate of a gift as given, the left could confirm its receipt. The "behavior" would have all the characteristics of a transfer. The testimony of both this and that hand, of the giving and receiving hand, would however belong to the same I; thus no change of ownership would occur—this testimony presupposes something that simply cannot be "seen," because the solid connection of both hands to the same body provides no reliable information about it. After he has described the action, Wittgenstein's gesture belongs to the dismissive kind that he uses to confront modern doubt from Descartes to Russell: "Well, and now what?" The only thing the reader can still doubt comes up in the counterquestion: "Is this still a philosophical way to ask a question?" It may be, however, that all of this can no longer be prescribed to the epoch that Descartes had begun by overtaxing the claims to "reality."

We have no account of Descartes and which gestures may have expressed his loss of a link to reality—after all, he didn't stand in front of an auditorium, didn't have a "constant companion" who listened to and watched him, all of which would have provided the Cartesian "school" with a livelier image. The most quoted grand master of English literature after Shakespeare, Samuel Johnson, did have such a proto-Eckermann in the shape of James Boswell, who became almost as famous through his protocol-like biography of Johnson. German literature is indebted to Johnson for the four-line poem that Goethe wrote in 1824 when he gave Johnson's *Dictionary* to his anglophile daughter-in-law Ottilie as a present: "Big books! Lots of knowledge! / Oh, what I will have to learn! / If it doesn't find its way into my head / Let it be in the book instead! [Dicke Bücher! Vieles Wissen! / Ach! Was werd ich lernen müssen! / Will es nicht in Kopf hinein, / Mag es doch im Buche sein!]." This is one justification for the fact that you don't only acquire books to read them. Boswell's *The Life of Samuel Johnson* appeared in 1791, but the time for its overbearing aesthetic taste had already (again) just passed. The philosophical image of Johnson takes on color above all in the scene that is of interest here, that of Boswell's departure from Harwich on his Grand Tour of Germany and Switzerland in 1764, the diary of which is invaluable because of his encounters with Voltaire and Rousseau. The pious Johnson had compelled his young friend to attend church in Harwich so that he could commend himself to the care of his Creator and Redeemer; this circumstance may have determined the concluding conversation after leaving the church. They spoke about Bishop Berkeley and his all-too-clever idealism: his denial of material reality. Boswell declared Berkeley's position—although one was convinced that there was something wrong with it—to be irrefutable. What would henceforth be called "Johnson's kick" then took place. Boswell writes that he will never forget the nimble reaction of the heavy-bodied Johnson as he kicked a large stone so forcefully that his foot rebounded from it, and then used this as evidence in the laconic style that elsewhere lent his aesthetic judgments their convincing nature: "I refute it *thus*." They then hugged each other upon parting.

One easily ruins both the pleasure and the sense of significance in this great scene if one inquires into the premises of its "school of thought." Was it Locke's primary quality of the "solidity" of bodies that determined Johnson's demonstration and passion? Or does the accent lie less on the dead resistance than on the lively force of "elasticity" that opposes the kick, like life against life? This all matters little, since Johnson is not a figure in the history of philosophy. What he presents, what he represents, is how the century's currents break upon the resistance of a temperament. The explanations that Johnson gives us belong to the same type in which he held his kick to be evidence. What is important is that we can ask ourselves why the "kick" convinces us so little. It is not because our philosophy no longer allows this demonstration. Rather, our experience has been enriched with elements that make it seem unwise, for instance, to film that scene from 1764, because if one did, it would be possible both to depict the rebounding Dr. Johnson and, in a slapstick version, to show a large Styrofoam stone flying away as though it were nothing and the bishop of Cloyne were right. We live in a world of simulation; this even allows the world to be adapted to philosophical "systems."

When the popular philosopher Christian Garve sought to compare

Kant's *Critique* [*of Pure Reason*] with Berkeley's denial of nature's reality, Kant was right to limit himself to the apotropaic gesture involved in the slightly amended spelling of the expression "Bei Leibe nicht! [My foot!]."

The Suspicion of Meaninglessness

Meaninglessness [*Sinnlosigkeit*] is an evil word. It names a reproach that seems to justify extremes. It is, therefore, also a dangerous word. Meaninglessness insinuates not only a lack but also a withholding, a robbing of what is essential, so that one would be completely justified in looking for a guilty party, if there were guilt.

The characterization of a condition as meaningless entails offering the loss of meaning as an explanation for the course of things, for how this condition arose; this description of things includes the notion that whatever could be lost had already existed and thus makes no utopian claims. And yet one has always had difficulty naming the positive countermovement to a loss of meaning. The relatively recent term "production of meaning" is rather ironic and signals a certain presumptuousness. One doesn't even have a name for awakening the illusion that what was once supposedly lost might one day be found again.

An expectation, however, that offers itself so globally and indeterminately is a threatening feature. Just as one repeatedly seeks representatives for a world worth destroying in order to be able to hit anything at all, one will also look for representatives of those to blame for this loss and, to their misfortune, will find them. Thus do fundamentalist ways of thinking come into being. They seem to offer something that has been lost by concentrating their destructive energy on the guilt for this loss. Since this is a typical procedure in history, one cannot shy away from posing the question of whether such meaninglessness doesn't, in fact, describe the privation of something that doesn't exist and, as something supposedly lost, never existed in the first place.

What can be described is how the suspicion of meaninglessness came into being. The era after the birth of Christ has a culture of contingency. This era is shaped by the fundamental thought that whatever exists doesn't have to be. This is not as self-evident as it sounds in the century where evolutionary thought is victorious. Christianity is, however, *also* a creation religion that, as such, lends the strongest of all possible justifications to what exists: the justification that comes from the will of its God. Without this, there would be nothing. Nevertheless, something pushed its way in front of the memory of the Bible's Genesis, something that constitutes the concentrated effective power of the New Testament's message: the fact that the world can be recalled, its apocalyptical determination for destruction, its due date for Final Judgment. There were those who, not lacking insight into the whole, didn't want to believe that *the same* God who had created the world now condemned it to ruin, as if it were the foolhardy, shoddy effort of someone else. But one could not have and hold the messianic hope of the coming of the Lord and the advent of the Kingdom of Heaven—the reason why one is ready for truly great sacrifices—without admitting the depravity of this still continuing world. When it first becomes clear what the meaninglessness of the world includes—namely, its being worthy of destruction—an answer to the following question falters due to the inner contradiction of its conception: What meaningful condition could have preceded this asserted state of the world and, again, what might follow upon its decay?

What then arose and could always be reanimated was a silent expectation, whose entire energy for action came from the certainty that the world could not be saved anyway, and that everything must therefore be expected from its destruction. It is pointless to ask whether in these situations such negative findings about the world are shared by all or many; what is decisive is that certainty about the invalidity of all things rages toward the immediate end. Meaninglessness appears as a mere displacement of meaning: what has been withdrawn from life and the world is found on the other side of the balance, next to the unnamable, what comes after.

This configuration can now also be read in the opposite direction. If the world becomes meaningless—whatever this may mean and as a result of whatever process—then the world arouses a wish for its destruction, an indeterminate rage at its continued existence and those in it. Because human life takes place in this world, meaning is denied to humanity and the world alike. The apocalyptic threat is transformed into the hope that what is suspected of being meaningless—if it were only destroyed—will let nothing arise or leave nothing behind other than what proves to be meaningful.

Only by naming signs of deficiency does one think to know what linguistic expressions containing the element "meaning" signify, as if nothing were more understandable. What a quandary it is when the accusatory handling of the expression "meaning" is asked about its own sense of responsibility. The admission "We don't know what we mean when we use the word 'meaning'" already appears to require fearlessness. And here as well, there is a technique of reversal: the impertinent demand to provide meaning, to satisfy the desire for meaning, to make good the losses of meaning, to bestow meaning could produce as its rhetorical effect of all things a dilemma. Sigmund Freud rightfully said that whoever asks for the meaning of life is sick. From this it follows that he must be healed, not satisfied; and if not healed, then consoled.

Whoever lacks meaning needs consolation. This is the only chance for himself and others that he doesn't fall prey to the indeterminate rage that can only vent itself on symbols and relies on searching for self-justifications: for representatives of what cannot be and cannot be as it is. Therefore, part of pursuing a public accusation of meaninglessness includes discriminating against consolation as well as against the skeptical counterquestion of what is meant.

The culture of contingency is the culture of a possible rage at the world, and its extreme value is to pursue the world's ruin. In an apocryphal Passion of Paul, it is the Roman emperor Nero (of all people) who is moved to blind fury when the apostle proclaims the burning of the world; when the Roman emperor thereupon turns the Christians into torches, he has them symbolically atone for the fact that they not only expect the end of the world but also ritually bring it about. What the Stoics taught as a natural process, namely, the depletion of fire as a productive power, the Christians are said here to have elevated to their agenda and subjected to their God's influence. Lying behind this is the notion that the world doesn't need to be; not only that it doesn't need to be as it is, but also that it doesn't need to be at all. The culture of contingency fosters what isn't self-evident: that what still is and appears to remain could just as well have been long gone. Schopenhauer will err when he says that the "admiration" of the world—which Plato spoke of as the origin of philosophy—is already identical to the "astonishment" that there is something rather than nothing at all.

For Schopenhauer, "the uneasiness that keeps the unstopping clock of metaphysics in motion is the consciousness that the nonbeing of this world is just as possible as its being." This idea would have been foreign to antiquity in all of its forms of thought. In Schopenhauer's formulation lies the suspicion that the world—even if one can narrate a plausible story of origin for its existence—so little satisfies the claim to meaning that it in no way hinders the flirtation with the possibility of its nonbeing. This is the point where all dissatisfaction finds its outlet, and no dissent can compare in seriousness with what it refers to.

It is simply false to think that if the meaninglessness of the world is driven far enough then its opposite must be ascertainable and worth striving for: the recoverability of what is supposedly lost—the meaning of the world and life. But there never was such meaning, and the demand for it originated on the foothills of the culture of contingency. The feeling that the world is meaningless does yet not imply that it might, in the end, be experienced as meaningful—under appropriately changed symptoms and conditions, by settling the problem of values, and by ending alienation. The only thing that supports describing the origin of the culture of contingency as coming from the Christian biblical syndrome is that in the best case, a world as cosmos is accepted in a self-evident manner as that which is and cannot *not* be, in fact, could not even be different than it is. As long as this notion was valid, no one could express it in this way. This is a language that can only be spoken after the fact. At most, metaphor makes it graspable: Even the world of the Stoics meets its demise (*ekpyrosis*), but only in order to rise again as the same world like the mythical Phoenix. For the Stoics, only the power that maintains the world needs recuperation; the cosmos doesn't need change. One can dream of retrieving this thought, one cannot tenably think it.

The statement "meaninglessness is felt regarding the world and life" is not descriptive. It is an instrument of confrontation. Insofar as the suspicion of meaninglessness is bound up with a question whose fate is to be unanswerable, it produces helplessness; and nothing is more helpful in confrontations than the helplessness of the other. Back when an entire arsenal of means for scaring the "bourgeoisie" was still available, it was relatively harmless to shock and shame it as incapable of bearing the naked truth. When this instrument's inventive richness was exhausted, there ensued a comprehensive attempt driven to the highest heights of theoretical abstraction to make the bourgeoisie guilty of any and everything: no defense in court that wouldn't have pointed the finger at an indeterminate horizon of guiltiness. In the best case, one preempted this situation through intelligent and complicated self-accusations. The generations of the shocked and guilty were followed by the generations of the confused. How should one answer those who would ask for meaning—the meaning of life, of history, of the state, of everything?

These people ask, however, because they know that the others cannot answer. They should at least know why they cannot answer and why they nevertheless are asked. To let confusion appear as a refusal to answer rhetorically distributes the burden in the dialogue of those who have been declared incapable of dialogue. Refusal, as the refusal of those who are owed something [*Gesollten*], provokes the pantomime of "rage at the world," with which the millennium appears to come to an end.

The Restlessness of the Spirits

"The principle of reason put an end to the peaceful rest of the spirits," Schopenhauer noted on the endpaper of his edition of the Eleatic fragments. Thus does one philosophically imagine the beginning of philosophizing. But doubting this image is also philosophical. Wasn't the principle of reason, wherever it may have begun, part of the repertoire of means employed to first gain the "peaceful rest of the spirits"? Wasn't it a way to attribute a bit more reliability and submissiveness to the world, reality, and things than is said to have been possible through the procedure of mere conjuring, ritual, and narration?

Nothing in history tends toward putting an end to the "peaceful rest of spirits"—which doesn't exclude that de facto it hasn't been put to an end here and there. For the most part, these ends were failures of the opposed effort to provide the spirits with something final.

What robbed the spirits of their supposed rest was above all the fact that the remedy with which they should have been calmed was indigestible. In the wake of Parmenides, the Eleatics, whose fragments Schopenhauer commented upon with the sentence quoted above, used drastic paradoxes of movement to try to prove the uniqueness of being at rest and its complete disjunction from nonbeing. But the paradoxes immediately infected what they were supposed to stabilize and demonstrated that the alternative between being and nonbeing was dissolvable, even tending toward nonbeing. Gorgias wrote a treatise that proved that there is nothing; if there actually were something, we wouldn't know anything about it; if we did know it, we couldn't say it. The first great calming of the spirits through the solidity of the one, unique being failed due to the excessiveness of its argumentative effort. In failure, however, the way was already prepared for a new round of calming down.

Perhaps the finest expression of this circumstance, one that contradicts

Schopenhauer, is that the most effective means of calming down to emerge from the series of ever more intolerable and indigestible remedies was Pyrrhonist skepticism's rule of abstinence. It is so enlightening that it belatedly makes things intelligible: in the dogmatic schools' unresolved conflict over their demonstrable contradictions, only the pacifiers [*die Sedative*] did battle.

A Loss of the Last Judgment

Of all the losses that have accompanied the debilitation of Christianity, the loss of that bit of faith about Jesus returning to judge the living and the dead is perhaps the most irreplaceable. Viewed as a threat, the Last Judgment disturbs theologians, since they think promises are "more effective advertising." To the extent they still speak of it, theologians have allegorized the Last Judgment as an inner coming to terms with guilt or as an external "redistribution" of debts. The Last Judgment, however, was originally anything but a threat. Insofar as it was supposed to cast away the guilty, it a fortiori gave those who suffered injustice their share back and more. The persecuted believers would be triumphant on the Last Day. And they could scarcely wait for it.

The perceptible lengthening of the waiting period not only reduced the certainty of those assured of their salvation; it also led to a fatal weakening of the idea of the Last Judgment. Inevitably, there arose the question concerning the intervening period between death and judgment and with it a dogmatic doubling of the Last Judgment into "particular" and "universal." Particular judgment already delivered the decision regarding salvation, universal judgment only publicly announced it. The Last Day was dedicated more to the history of salvation than to the decision of salvation—a first inner-dogmatic moment of "theodicy," since God, without being asked, would account for his "total artwork [*Gesamtkunstwerk*]" called the world. The solution to the greatest enigma. With the privatization of the first part of the Last Judgment (which, according to the orthodox model, should exclude every "provisional arrangement" of an indecisive, Hades-like condition), the "consolation" of those inconsolable about history was degraded to a mere spectacle. Divine judgment was moved so close to the world that theological acts of violence were no longer necessary in order to draw divine judgment into the world: to turn conscience into the figure of the world's judge.

Moralists have never thought much about all this talk of judgment. From their perspective, fear of punishment or hope of reward could only annihilate freedom in the face of the moral law. It seemed to be the pinnacle of Enlightenment reason to eliminate all the conditions for the Last Judgment: the certainty of the divine judge's existence, the belief in immortality, the finitude of the world and history. To be sure, moral-political progress would not provide justice to those who had suffered injustice; rather, it would compensate the kind or class he belonged to in his stead. The people who now entered the kingdom of heaven were different than those who had earned it, but through an artifact of identity raised to a higher degree, somehow still the same. Hadn't parents from time immemorial been assuaged for their lot through the lot of their children?

It was evidently easier to compensate the suffering of injustice through a substitute for judgment than it was to compensate for the guilt of having caused injustice through "charity" and "reparations" of all kinds, which had to invent equivalents for misfortune; to the extent that extremely miserable things were eliminated through organized and legal measures, it became ever more difficult to believe in such equivalence. A remnant of the *ius talionis*—the reflexive vengeance of "an eye for an eye, a tooth for a tooth"—persists in all types of "coming to terms": sinners who do penance by tormenting and torturing themselves generally no longer really know for what trespasses it serves them right. Herein lies the infinite ability to transgress the legalism that only wants to see recognized, legally defined deeds punished, while moralism commands holding the conviction that deeds possess only a factual expression—thus also, in certain circumstances, no expression at all.

This "in certain circumstances [*unter Umstände*]" is the driving force restlessly working to transgress the border of every inner jurisdiction. To say that we are all sinners would be a relatively harmless admission (one that might recall certain moments in life and entire "pasts"), if it weren't for the reservations about those "circumstances" that first give birth to the complete seriousness of a malice that can intensify up to the unforgivable "sin against the [Holy] Spirit." No one has ever said what this sin might be, but the consciousness that it could exist—if only the opportunity, the provocation, the "temptation" in the highest sense were present—persists. Part of the consciousness of contingency imposed on every life is being this person instead of the other, existing here and today instead of there and tomorrow, and finally existing at all instead of simply not existing—

one who wasn't born would have nothing to come to terms with. Divine judgment would be merciless if each person with his or her convictions had to take responsibility for every *possible* existence. Ergo, the overpowering glory of martyrdom in Christian history: dying for truth or innocence approaches the absolute purity of not having been born in the first place, while also taking away a good part of the Last Judgment's latitude in inquiring into what is still possible in living on. It is not an accident that in a footnote in his late treatise *Religion Within the Limits of Mere Reason* (1793), Kant deviated from the comforting biblical scene in which the Son of Man will be the judge of man in order to talk about the court of judgment held by the Holy Spirit as "the actual judge of humanity." Kant, however, parenthetically adds the philosophical point that levels everything once again: "before the court of their conscience [*vor ihrem Gewissen*]." Here there is only one person imaginable for whom the "benefit of a late birth" does as little good as any other facticity of birth. He must "come to terms" not only with a past or his past but also with the possible present times in which he could just as well exist, and finally with the possible worlds that do not but could exist. The abyss of subjunctives first produces sinners as well as the wish for a judgment that would no longer accept any coincidences and circumstances—not even the mitigating circumstances of the facticity that produces all human compassion as the feeling of guilt not about deeds and convictions but rather about sparing the obligations and impulses toward them. Perhaps this lost Last Judgment, this world tribunal that has been forgotten in the age after Christ or cancelled by the "Enlightenment," belongs to what we have been undeservedly spared, insofar as no pastor courts unpopularity by still reminding people of it?

The philosopher's court of judgment of the Holy Spirit makes one wonder: isn't the irremovable uncertainty connected to the contingency of being (how would another person have survived this under other conditions?) horrible enough to satisfy the autonomous law of reason? Doesn't it lead to self-made trial situations, to simulations of the tempting case of emergency [*Ernstfall*], whose result is always the desired outcome of self-confirmation that can only be registered in the subjunctive mood: if we were put in the circumstances of guilty others—fathers and forefathers, inhabitants of other zones and continents, subjects of other obligations and systems—then acquittal could not be refused us.

One forgets the failed great test during the state of exception of early Christianity's anticipation of the end of time, which expected the baptized to lead a sinless lifestyle for only a few days—and immediately produced the problem of delay, of whether one could and must be baptized again if one failed to remain sinless. The Pharisee Paul knew what he was doing with the message of salvation when he defined "justification" as the acquittal that is freely given during the Last Judgment through identification with the resurrected one: liberation from the unrealizable nature of divine law as the epitome of a promise. In the philosopher's court of the Holy Spirit as the "actual judge," there can be no acquittals given as presents, even when the accused no longer calls himself "sinner," but rather is one who owes something indefinite to all the world and many ages. To this extent, it was everything but an act of "secularization" to load up Dasein with its facticity as an unshakeable long-term guilt; and one understands the fascination of theologians through this philosophy of existence that, for a now indeterminate promise of salvation, grabs hold of equally indeterminate sinners by their predetermined consciousness of never having earned or being able to earn it, of not being one, who like Friedrich Hebbel, had to scream: ". . . why am I as I am? The most hideous thing!"

The analytical description of "existence" neither replaced nor renewed the old "sinner"; it created another guilty [or: indebted, *Schuldigen*] person of unequally more horrible insolvency. For this person, not only is there factually no redemption; there can be none. All of this was still pronounced with theoretical noncommitment and offered for use when one still had no good idea about its usability for the enormity of people doing what no one believed they were capable of, presumably not even they themselves. The simplification that says it was a matter of bloodthirsty beasts running around in search of victims, anticipating being glutted, until someone handed the beasts their prey, is already an auxiliary construction for tests of innocence, since it is easy to *not* diagnose bloodthirsty bestiality in oneself, even with the most thorough investigation. But it is precisely here that it becomes clear how harmless it is to compare the Last Judgment with mere introspection of conscience. The philosopher's court of judgment doesn't bring the factual [*faktisch*] subject before the tribunal of conscience but rather de-factualizes it through the *potentialis* of worlds it had no need to live in. This is, indeed, a limit-concept of "justice" but not a fiction: all humanity is based upon a capacity of consciousness that is not at all self-evident—not *having* to think of oneself as the person one is, but rather thinking of every other person as the person one *could* be. The biblical concept of the "neighbor [*Nächsten*]" first comes into being when the limit-concept is replaced by spatial metaphorics: one's neighbor is the person whom one only by chance happens not to be. This circumstance is what allows the "need for the Last Judgment" to continue and to remain unfulfilled—and in the balance of needs, something that can't be fulfilled is always a risky proposition.

A good part of what goes on in the sciences has to do with the loss of the Last Judgment. It is no longer the case that world history is seen as the Last Judgment of the world, and the historian's job is to keep it at bay. But history illustrates the entire dimension in which, at least for anyone who doesn't shun the sight, there could have been the "temptations" that Satan in the New Testament brought in an exemplarily concentrated form to the Son of Man after forty days of fasting in the desert, that is, after the test of holiness! It would trivialize this unbelievable part of the Bible (also looking toward the agony in the Garden of Gethsemane), if one wanted to pretend that Jesus surviving Satan's attack determines his inability to be tempted as the Son of God. Rather, this scene of temptation is written as a reproach to all who would like to measure up to a judgment they no longer need to believe in—whose "idea," however, is not spared them.

The biblical injunction "Judge not!" is a conditional command: it is another who will judge. Or has already judged, in what John regards as the secrecy of the always fruitlessly expected great act of salvation: "The prince of this world has already judged," and whoever believes this "does not come before the court of judgment," but already has eternal life. This consolation for the eschatological false expectation had as little effect as the Pauline "acquittal" throughout one and a half millennia. The post-Christian loss of the Last Judgment is as difficult to get over as the inner Christian postponement of the Last Judgment during its temporary ban. World history arises as the history of *civitas dei* [City of God] to prove that the delay of the Last Judgment is not in vain. World history thereby inevitably absorbs the world's Last Judgment, for otherwise the counterproof would degrade the *mora finis* [delay of the end], which had been begged for and granted, to a carrying out of salvation, to a postmessianic as-if-nothing-had-been. The judge cannot refuse judgment, and if he delays it, he has to ensure that, in delaying judgment, he does not cause a new disaster. The historian thus has his interim office and does nothing explicitly except what he was always implicitly doing anyway: judging history. Even as a startled historian of the present, he looks for the conditions in which "contemporary history" would not have been able to occur—or, if he inclines toward determinism, he looks for the assurance that such determinants no longer exist. During his imprisonment in the tower, Sir Walter Raleigh threw the manuscript of his *History of the World* into the fire; he punished his queen and judges by withdrawing the proof of how they fit into the whole. He refused judgment at the juncture where he, as prisoner, was still judge. Anatole France, who cites this as an unforgivable act, intended the four volumes of his *Histoire contemporaine*, history that still affects its actors, as the opposite pole to the precedence given to ancient history, which can produce knowledge and do justice precisely because it no longer injures or benefits any particular person. These are the limits to the pagan obstinacy of history in the face of the command "Judge not!"—which doesn't even concede that the waning of the Christian God could have left behind the loss of the Last Judgment as a trauma.

Aversion to Knowledge

The great enigma of the closing second millennium is and will perhaps remain the growing aversion to science. As with other changes of mood and valuation, this discontent bestows itself with a decisiveness that it doesn't have. It names culprits and deeds, evidence and witnesses, facts and factors of a disaster that supposedly came from science, or is still to come, and threatens to culminate in the destruction of the world, the downfall of humanity, and the devastation of nature. To call this an exaggeration is already an imposition; any fraction of what is estimated here as a whole would already be disastrous enough.

It makes one suspicious, however, when the same science that is supposedly preparing humanity's downfall at the same time enabled the explosion of humanity's fertility, which could lead, without any great weapons, to a permanent conflict for survival with clubs and stones. This explosion rests upon good deeds that no one openly dares to belatedly accuse science of and to ban from it after the fact: where and according to what criterion should one let another die by curbing known life-saving possibilities within knowledge's field of competence by simply refusing their revelation—for mothers and infants, in the case of countless diseases and epidemics, in the case of the most amazing augmentation of food production? Humanity could be less numerous than it is, less threatened by itself and the elementary conflict that not only concerns the military superpowers but also anyone anywhere who still has something that the next person walking by needs or thinks to need.

In the fourteenth century, humanity almost died out from the plague that ate its way from eastern Asia to western Europe—but only almost, since more than half of the inhabitants of the then known world survived. The probability of such an event now repeating itself under the conditions of science is low, and this probability is not quantitatively offset by the overkill of weapon arsenals.

One can, however, neither defend science by citing its protective accomplishments nor condemn it for what it threatens. Also the middle road of planning science's successes more exactly and avoiding its failures more efficiently will more likely paralyze than motivate it; and even in the best-case scenario, this strategy will not remove the suspicion that science could at any time and anywhere do what it wouldn't do factually in the given moment due to the prevailing perspective or the constraint of laws. Expressed somewhat flippantly, it would look something like this: you can't get rid of "know-how." I want to express it more drastically: humanity's new problem would be an enormous, worldwide black market (with all the side effects and consequences of this phenomenon) in everything that didn't openly exist.

The point of arguing along these lines is to make evident the improbability that the frustration with science could have something to do with the acute threats that hover over the world and, without a doubt, would certainly look different without science, but for the same reason would also not assume another dimension. Essentially, it is more amazing how one *doesn't* argue in the manifest instances of this frustration than how the positions in this dispute have actually been formed and formulated.

Truth as a goal of the highest rank, as an absolute good, one that in our tradition is, in the final instance, identical with God—as an argument, this notion is dead. I do not doubt that this has something to do with what Nietzsche gave the mythic name of the death of God. Lonely speakers in remote academic ceremonies timidly still say now and again that science has sworn itself to truth and has to accept no limitations in keeping this vow.

That science goes to work for truth is not a lie, but also not the entire truth. It may sound like a petty correction if I say that under the ideal of seeking truth through research, science only opposed error and made itself into a means of enlightenment against a world of supposed or genuine prejudices. One can clarify this with a simple example. As the secretary of the French Academy of Sciences in the first half of the eighteenth century put on the record, the explanation that the so-called "thunderstones" found on all ocean beaches were the remains of extinct sea creatures ([cephalopod] belemnites) was less a new insight—which, like every other insight, would have been welcomed as an augmentation of our knowledge of the world—and more the elimination of an error, of an old and mythically tinged prejudice. It was less the triumph of a new truth than access to the possibility of another explanation, one that could not be proven, that didn't even need to be proven.

The constitution of a system of truths mattered less than the dissolution of a system of "prejudices," whose general characteristic was to reckon with powers in the world that didn't belong to the world and seemed to not adhere to its laws—powers that hurled lightning and thunderstone to punish the sinner or to test the just person; in any case, powers that acted with a definite intention toward this or that person. It was a world in which the target was hit. In this way, one was to break out, piece by piece, from a given, preexisting system that didn't appear to let humanity possess itself and its rational faculty; this could occur, however, only when one had a "substitute" to offer for each piece and each position of this system, a replacement that was stronger, or at least appeared so, and thus did not also have to immediately be "the truth."

One doesn't say it, but the creation of doubt was, for the most part, knowledge's soundest accomplishment.

The effort that fueled this intention and brought humanity into ever greater movement and enthusiasm was too great to be limited to the genuine model of the "Enlightenment" agenda. Expressed differently and more simply: the system of "error" was too small to limit this theoretical process, once it had been set in motion, to the mere substitution of "prejudices." Insights were gained that could no longer be related to anything old; they had crossed the border of the old world just as the explorers of unknown continents had done. And here the connection between truth and freedom—which constitutes the heart of our tradition, including the biblical tradition—began to fray: emancipation from error became an unclear goal.

Science is truth or acts as if it were, as long as it has to do with a demonized antagonist, regardless of how this demonization occurs. To the extent that the opposition between science and error is lost—since scientific results no longer discover any corresponding prejudices—the acute urgency of being emancipated from something wanes. It was a symptom of great clarity that the outbreak of discontent with science was accompanied by a "last attempt" of people living from science to maintain the impression that one was dealing with an opponent who had become ever more secretive and underhanded—by simply adding the epithet "critical" to all possible disciplines and to science in general. To detect this opponent one needed the complete craftiness [*Raffinement*] of exposing and calling into question, of penetrating the depths of the soul and the depths of narrowed consciousness.

Dubbing science "critical" was an act of self-help against the absolutism of truth that no longer seemed to have anything opposed to it and no longer opposed anything. At the same time, it was not only a matter of backgrounds but also, in the background, it was a matter of privileging certain disciplines that seemed to still know the enemy. And it concerned the discrimination of other disciplines that supposedly already revolved in the empty space outside the gravitational field of earthly conditions. The competition of interests as a last dualism within science itself could only strengthen the frustration, the discontent with the lack of realities that had something to do with the paucity of certainty and orientation— and not only with the uncertain careers of theoreticians.

This is not *the* end, because there can no longer be a renunciation of science. With so many effects of science (both good and bad) already in the world, only science can be the instrument for coming to terms with itself. For the time being, this is *an* end: an end to the exuberant expectation, to approaching omnipotence and limitlessness. At any rate, helplessness—not only in this area—can easily be confused with a proximity to demise. If this is an end, where was the beginning? Before all the fear from the threat of side effects, where did one begin to see the element of an essential atrophy of motivation and dynamism in the modern process of knowledge and then relate it to the genuine function of an antagonism between prejudice and knowledge?

I mentioned Nietzsche's mythic talk of the death of God and connected it to the dying-off of a relation to truth. If there is something to this, it is most likely in Nietzsche that one should be able to find a beginning to the entirely nonmythical state of affairs, in which the old function of truth is neither self-evident nor atemporal, and that therefore it cannot always be expected to readily function.

Nietzsche's own dissatisfaction with scientific truth doesn't cover this result. He was already too clearly pursuing a new dimension of aesthetic fulfillment along the lines of the *Gesamtkunstwerk*. Dissatisfaction lacks diagnostic precision, because one imagines one has something better in mind. As the nineteenth century drew to a close, Nietzsche saw "science's youthful appeal" not yet waning, but nevertheless already relying on a contrast that left him uncertain as to whether it was a constitutive part of the modern scientific syndrome: "Searching for truth still has the appeal that truth everywhere stands out strongly against error, which has grown gray and boring; this appeal is increasingly subsiding." One still lives in "the youthful age of science," Nietzsche continues, and pursues truth like a beautiful girl. It will grow old. What then? Here the fate of science is still bound to the metaphor of human life and the inevitable fading of erotic appeal.

Side Effects of the Need for Meaning

The suspicion that the world might be devoid of meaning, or might have forfeited the meaning it once possessed, weighs heavy upon those who, owing to a careless career choice (or for some other reason), are pestered by impatient people for information and remedies.

Leaving aside the question of how expensive good advice may be after one accepts this challenge, another question has to be asked: if one of the meaning-seekers were to strike it rich, to bring to light the desired meaning, to restore the lost meaning, what would success, or its mere consequences, look like?

Only a utopia expert could deal with the jubilation of the first days of success, the satisfaction and the accolades during the distribution of the wealth of meaning. What I plan to do is something more sober. One of our modern world's more or less unexpected, tormenting to painful experiences is that its most beautiful achievements drag behind a train of unpopular things that we have learned to call "side effects." Some people take this to be an understatement, others as a set of burdensome footnotes to the main text. If one presupposes recovering the meaning of being and the world, of life and history, what would have to be an expected side effect of this otherwise ecological progress?

Certain preliminary studies on this question are permitted by epochs and formations, where one thought one knew the meaning of being and the world rather precisely, and, much to the envy of romantic successors, seemed to live off this possession of meaning. The rediscovery of the Middle Ages, for example, has been shot through with the nostalgic supposition that precisely this interim world between antiquity and modernity, a world now disparaged as dark, was in reality an age abounding in meaning and fulfilled lives, since one knew why one was living, if only briefly. The keywords of such an abundance of meaning are familiar: a world set in motion by a benevolent hand; directed by the same hand toward a final goal of fulfilling its history; the being of every single creature purposefully classified in this whole with a just share of burden and pleasure; and at the end of the Final Judgment, everything that could not yet be classified under the rubrics of the criteria for meaning would be accounted for and clarified. It would then be clear why some had to suffer and the others got off well.

To assume that one lives in a meaning-driven world where every event must in principle be open to examination regarding its "why" and "whither"—even if it does not always willingly provide such information—is not without its risks. If visible suffering befalls one in such a world, one can scarcely avoid asking oneself, and especially having others ask, what secret, reprehensible act led to this punishment. If the world is ordered in a thoroughly meaningful manner, unfortunate people are not merely unfortunate—they are also responsible for it. Although scrutinizing reason has scored a series of enlightenments and spectacular achievements, we have to this day not entirely escaped the shabby quotidian wisdom that one is better off hiding certain stigmatizing diseases and afflictions so as to avoid the diffuse suspicion that someone—parents or forefathers or oneself—must have sinned in a corresponding fashion, even when one uses a more modern means to express this thought.

There is, therefore, another side of the coin to a world pregnant with meaning: one can know or one thinks one knows or one is urged to know who is currently guilty of what, who is to blame for what. It was my early childhood history that let me dream, but someone other than myself was responsible for the fact that my childhood went the way it did, and for how it now pursues me in my dreams, so that I even need the help of others, if only in order to understand the symbolism of my dreams.

In a meaningful world, there have to be hints, orientation points, signposts, instructions, signs, signatures. Every herb must show what a decoction of it might be good for. No one is nature's favorite without a reason; and whoever is nature's favorite understands above all how to read the signs (also those found on foreheads, like the ineffable Lavater) and holds judgment even before Judgment Day arrives.

Arranged in such a way, the world becomes, as one of its side effects, a reality of possible reverse conclusions: whoever rides in a carriage must have been good or at least still be able to become good; whoever has to walk has truly earned it, or his only chance of still being able to compare with the good lies in this detour. One can narrate the story of the meaningful and meaning-driven world—as utopists have always admitted—only in the form of a fairytale. Meaning always also means that what each and every thing is actually about becomes visible. One has to be ready to bear this fact.

In January 1939, the invaluable Alfred Polgar published in the *Pariser Tageszeitung* an ironic inversion of human history's first fratricide as an attempt to interpret the fate incomprehensible to so many German emigrants: being marked once again in their respective countries of refuge. They were not spared the mistrust that comes precisely from trusting meaning: the person who suffers this fate thinks there must be something that gives fate the right to treat him or her in this way. The inverted myth consists in only two sentences and needs no further reflection: "If he had fled in the face of his brother Cain's murderous intentions, Abel would as an emigrant have had to endure bitter vexation. All his life, he would have wandered the world with the mark of Abel on his forehead."

If a world where the mere *presumption* that this and that thing must occasionally be meaningful (especially when this occurs systematically on a mass scale), if such a world already appears to be one struck with this meaning and the suspicion that it needs to be implemented, then it is not difficult to imagine how a world would have to look where *certainty* of its bestowed meaning existed in each and every thing. The tormented person would say to himself: everything has its meaning, and this meaning will be revealed one day. But he would keep this consolation to himself, for it could have cruel repercussions for him.

Perhaps we should cultivate not only a rage at the meaninglessness of the world, but also a bit of fear in the face of the possibility that some day it could be replete with meaning. If Anaximander's enigmatic primal insight from the middle of the sixth century BCE, the oldest reported fragment of early Greek philosophy, is that things have to pay each other punishment and penance for their nefariousness as firmly decreed by time, then perhaps we have to be happy that no more than this was bequeathed to us. It could have contained something about the grounds for judgment and evidences of such a rule of meaning over the world.

The meaninglessness of history, discharged in the fragmentation of its worthiest surviving elements, has protected us from one of the attempts to put into action the claim to meaning. The degree to which we are susceptible to such things—and, indeed, how we can't be any different— was demonstrated when in the first year after the greatest catastrophe of meaning to date, precisely this dictum of Anaximander's was subjected to an interpretation by Heidegger—luckily, one that has remained highly incomprehensible and philologically improbable.

Remnants of the Unattainable

Among language's amazing inventions, one can count the invention of the unsayable; not only as a statement of failure in what is essential and considerable, but also as the marking of what has been affected by language's self-limitation: the marking of the "individual" and the "one," each on opposite ends of the scale of all that exists, as Neoplatonism first postulated them.

When one situates this as a clue in a larger framework, then language also partially states a phenomenon of greater scope and diversity: the unsayable is only a part of the unattainable. Even more important: this possesses a great historical versatility; it can be taken as a characteristic of fundamental changes.

When something that up until now had been thought to be unattainable is nevertheless attained, the vacancy in the systematics of consciousness results not in reassurance but reallocation. One can express this in a more topographical image: if the unattainable is lost in *one* direction, a substitute is sought in another direction. The unattainable has a preciousness that must be distributed across reality in determinate quantities, even though this can be a matter of mere fictions.

Using up this quantity of the unattainable is more alarming than a decline of something else, because such depletion produces the mass inertia of consciousness that can be called with great indeterminateness "boredom" and is a source of countless evils. One only has to imagine what it would be like in all sports with measurable achievements if it could be proven from physiological or physical reasons that certain measured values mark the extreme of what can be achieved, so that the incessant objection about what is unattainable "only for now" and "in given conditions" would no longer be possible. The consequence would be an immobilization of great dimensions. Mind you, the opposite assurance of the physical or physiological kind—that is, that there is still leeway in what can be attained—would have only a moderately stimulating value and not the attractive value of what has been declared unattainable for a reason, even if not a compelling one.

One can easily elucidate this situation with a topic that is historically removed but filled centuries of history after Christ with countless disputes replete with victims: the concept of mercy [*Gnade*]. In this concept lies the notion that mercy is not equivalent to merit, whose corresponding term would be something like the opposite of punishment (that is, reward). In mercy there is always something that cannot be attained by effort. On the other hand, the thought that nothing depends on the person in question and his or her qualities, merits, and efforts, but rather that everything depends on the eternal and unfathomable will of the one bestowing mercy—this thought proved unbearable. How does one find justification, a justification that is unattainable and yet so necessary?

There is always an answer that avoids having absolute reservations. Only a few are chosen, but no one can know for sure that he or she doesn't belong to them. Whatever can only be a gift or mercy possesses its own unattainableness in relation to all solicitation, which Kant liked to call the solicitation of favor. But one also finds an either-or here; there is no partial justification. Late and belatedly, however, the institution of purgatory did insert something like partial justification, because the finality of the decision proved to be unbearable.

Space and time are the modern dimensions of the unattainable. Kant has shown that applying the categories of understanding to sensuous material renders something like the forms of outer and inner sense, space and time, necessary; the notion, however, that it had to be precisely these forms could not be proven and had to be accepted as a fact about how the human faculty of knowledge is organized. Phenomenology took the next step, at least with respect to time. It saw the essential structure of consciousness adequately dimensioned in the essential structure of the consciousness of time. Phenomenology, however, wasn't successful in demonstrating that space also essentially belongs to intentionality.

Both forms of organizing the contents of consciousness can, however, be equally described through the relation between attainability and unattainability. In the case of time and space, one can always declare that certain positions in finite time are attainable; but for each of these points in space and time, a horizon of the unattainable is essentially maintained and remains inexhaustible. In this fundamental relation, the intentionality of consciousness formally represents itself as still independent from the determinateness of factual objects in a world.

At first, infinity was a metaphysical category of a rather negative quality; then a theological one, and as such positive; after this, it became a cosmological category that was copied from the theological one as positive, but in so doing lost out and returned to the indeterminateness of its original metaphysical significance. Next, infinity became a central category of the philosophy of history and its focus on progress; finally, in phenomenology it became the self-determination of theoretical work as infinite. Although infinite work cannot clearly be qualified as positive (since by definition it simply doesn't get closer to its final goal), it does create in relation to its starting point the impression of a steadily growing distance and thus of increasing returns. The unattainable is the undertow of things attainable and remains untouched by them.

Space seemed to offer the safest haven for preserving the unattainable. And not only and primarily outer space; already on earth, the supposed edges of the populated world were for centuries considered to be the limits of what is accessible, the pillars of Hercules as gateways into expanses from which there was certainly no return and thus no information. Even the curiosity simultaneously unleashed and confirmed in the age of discoveries left the reserves of *terra incognita* untouched: the great primeval forests, the great deserts, both poles, the peaks of the highest mountains. One shouldn't forget that the exhaustion of the last enclaves of the unattainable on earth is not yet a full century old, like reaching the pole, and it is not even decades since the highest mountain summits were reached. This occurred almost simultaneously with the change in the perspective into outer space, where limits of finality appeared to have been drawn, and only fantasists could believe that even these limits would be crossed. One might argue that the actual breaking open of these limits in the decade of manned space travel is relatively minor—almost unimportant in the proportions of the solar system alone—yet the procedure of leaving the earth loses the sanction or the odium of unattainability.

Should the unattainable thereby be crossed out from consciousness's table of categories? At least in the case of time, there is still a dimension where the unattainable has been annulled once and for all: the past. Using the example of nobility, Arnold Gehlen has shown that nobility gains social quality to the extent that it has forfeited its function and ability to expand. Nobility assumes the preciousness of a substance that can no longer proliferate and, according to the conditions of its origin, could only be produced in the past. Can this notion be extended or even transferred as a whole to our relation to the past?

Gehlen applied the category of unattainability to the vitality of our relation to antiquity. In 1963—in the decade of the promised reaching of the moon—Gehlen sharply expressed this antithesis with one of his most pregnant sentences: "Precisely because we are about to occupy the moon, we cling to the earth of Attica." The connection between the past and unattainability is all the more evident, the more precisely the exhaustible size of a respective stock can be registered. One weakness of archeology may be the overestimation of its ability to unearth new discoveries. Only literary or musical artworks have their reality exclusively in reproduction (a reproduction that can take place at any time); only secondarily (through their performative interpretation) can they be endowed with the preciousness of uniqueness. After the deaths of their creators, plastic artworks possess the fixed quantity of his or her oeuvre. Although techniques of the plastic arts give the impression of being able to repeat, at any time, forms and contents that have once been invented and developed, the singularity of the handwriting, the principal recognizability of the original is, on the contrary, essential to them.

Beyond all thoughts of imitation and copying, the presupposition of an impossible return of the same remains wherever significance has been attained. The reason for this lies not only in the nonrepeatability of a situation or of individuality, but also in the logic of "position" in the context of a process embracing all individuals; in this process, art indeed produces art and is learned from what currently exists, but it also rebels against this and can define its own claim to being what can't be anticipated precisely through what is already there. The dating of the work characterizes its singularity still within the singularity of its authorship.

Attempts not only to make art *for* all (which art would like to do for a long time) but also to let it be made *by* all fail not primarily due to a lack of knowledge or a lack of will on the part of those who should be expected to renounce all originality. These attempts already fall apart with the thought of massive overproduction; no one would have time and desire to even take note of art, since one would be completely taken up with one's own share of its production. The basic romantic idea that all should not only be critics but also authentic producers of art loses sight of one thing: the need for a public that represents the other side of production and alone can satisfy production's need to maintain its determination of offering pleasure to the other people, to those who cannot or do not want to find pleasure in the process of production. These people fortuitously have other public or private goals and duties.

The absolutism of art always shies away from admitting that there can and must be people who want to connect or identify their life only marginally with the business of art—or perhaps not at all. Whatever claims to be or to become absolute cannot notice the fact that one attitude is to not notice this "absolute." The unattainable that would like to share its preciousness with everyone, that swings up or bends down to the obligatory attainable, can only register the following with reluctance or malice: what is attainable is no longer interesting.

With respect to the unattainable of the past, one will also have to consider that nature in its evolutionary procedure includes the extinction and disappearance of species and types. It is only an experience of the most recent times that lost early forms of living animal types can be regained. For example, Przewalski's Horse, an Asian wild horse that was found in Dzungaria [northwestern China] in 1879–80 and could be taken as the equivalent of the extinct Tarpan horse. The case of the okapi proves that legendary or even unbelievable animal types actually existed, and that they could be found and bred in captivity.

The Last of All Cult Victims: Boredom

As soon as entire nations are "educated" and their great possessions are presented to them in cult forms, boredom becomes rampant—and with it the duty to endure the boredom. Again and again, the degree of unbearability is connected to an ancient ritualistic suspicion: it is precisely the enormity of the sacred that is unbearable. And at the same time: the ability to endure the sacred confirms the survivor's being honored in the aura of the sacred object. The boredom involved in the game of cult consecration [*Weihekultspiellangweile*] becomes the institution that "the best" go through in order to establish and make known that they are the best.

Scarcely was the Kingdom of Versailles [i.e., the German Empire, proclaimed in the Hall of Mirrors at the Palace of Versailles in 1871] founded, when the need became manifest to find the condensed kernels of one's own cultivation of consciousness precisely in the new cult of art. David Friedrich Strauß had proposed the triad of German dramas: Lessing's *Nathan the Wise*, as well as Goethe's *Faust* and *Iphigenia in Tauris*. The theater critic [Theodor] Fontane, bored during a performance of just this *Iphigenia* at the Berlin Royal Theater on May 9, 1874, reacted to the recently deceased Strauß's idea with a casual "For all I care," followed by a just as definite, "But: . . . if this should happen, then the apparatus that shows us these things must become a different one." Had he overlooked the boredom that humanity had suffered from no less than if it were hunger since the time when there no longer was the "biogram" of unbroken rules of behavior for this one organism? Had he overlooked that this boredom in the discipline of cultures had become the last and finest sacrifice that a public could still bring to its gods?

Admittedly, the priests were not allowed to show that they too were bored. The actor, Herr Wünzer, who was about to leave the stage, played in this performance "as if he were already gone," and the Thoas [king of Scythia] played by the often admired Herr Berndal "showed signs of being infinitely bored." Not even and especially not the public could afford this, if it wanted to do justice to its national function.

The irony imposed on the unvindictive critic Fontane was that already on the thirty-first of the same month he had to acknowledge the same retiring Herr Wünzer in the new staging of *Hamlet*—which unfortunately didn't entirely fit in the national agenda—"Only Herr Wünzer was good (Ghost)." One would like to know whether this reviewer had a reading public that could be reached by a punch line delayed over three weeks.

Names Prescribe Burdens and Losses

Names direct us. Especially in the space where no one feels entirely at ease—even if no one has been cut open [*aufgeschnitten*]—names give the impression that they explain something.

In distant Canada, a person [the endocrinologist Hans Hugo Bruno Selye] uses six letters to invent a handy expression that names the strain of the world that presses on us all but obviously hasn't quite crushed us. No one knows exactly what it means: "stress." And yet everyone immediately begins to examine themselves and their condition to see whether *this* is the thing that has robbed them of the full desire for the world and everything else. One doesn't need to ask one's doctor. In situations of uncertainty, all diagnose themselves; all are their own wise gods. Unlike laboratory results, which so often disappoint us, there are no negative reactions. Whoever doesn't have what is designated by the new name is to blame. He leaves the army of those whom the Zeitgeist favors.

A decade later one reads with a vague recollection and slight disapproval that a researcher other than the distant Selye has found out or claims—which, in this case, amounts to the same thing—that "stress" is nothing but the bundle of stimuli and demands that keep life going; fending off and refusing this bundle, he writes, produces a generation of tired and lethargic moochers on other generations.

It will be difficult to elucidate how often during a lifetime one can be redirected by new names for one's condition. The names always possess certain additions to the rules of behavior: whether one should relax or rebel is often attached to different rules of behavior for one and the same result.

One day someone discovers that "frustration" is the perfect name for what one has or lacks. One insists that everything has to have meaning: whatever one does or what happens to one or what one perceives of the world in the range of words and images. If the proof of meaning is not delivered or otherwise recognizable, then one reserves the right not only to *be* against it but also to become *manifest* against it: generally by signing something that someone else has written, someone whom one doesn't know, but who obviously understands exactly how to say it, as one would have never been able to oneself.

What is amazing is that these names completely lack vividness. The old rhetorical maxim that images are most powerful in directing human opinions seems to fail. These days, a wild connection between foreign words and indefinable results proves to be stronger, because it suggests something shaped by science and thus also the hint of a guaranteed explanation of what it is about. We still do not know that we have begun to despise science, because we learn in this way to "experimentally" ascertain how science offers its slave service to everything and everyone: to the vague need as well as to the curiosity about oneself, to the dull sense of feeling sorry for oneself as well as to the complex of all discordant moods and dissatisfactions. One is to feel sorry for all those who work on their beautiful choice of names and theories for enjoyment—for who desires an explanation for the fact that he feels good now and again? For the fact that he knows and perceives enjoyment?

The observation that there is too little nominal material for pleasure and such rich nominal material for emotional frustration and cerebral uneasiness is not first made with the arrival of trendy foreign words. Even a vocabulary that hasn't been enriched by imported words shows the exact same disproportion and, thereby, betrays that searching for the name is neither an issue of today's day nor will it be of tomorrow's.

One day one finds oneself in a "midlife crisis" and then regrettably realizes only a while later that according to the most recent definition of "midlife" one does not yet or, worse still, no longer comes into consideration for this syndrome of an incomprehensible, deplorable state of affairs in oneself. The realization of not having been there and no longer being able to be in midlife is worse than the other one: a real relapse into the unnamed normality of the ups and downs and about-faces in the course of life. For this, one may immediately take part in the endemically rampant loss of meaning. It is open to everyone all the time.

The search for lost meaning busies us so much that perhaps some day someone will write six volumes about it. This length, this thoroughness, this industriousness arouses the suspicion that maybe the meaning of the loss of meaning is to keep us busy. Wanting to reach the peak of a lack of respect is also truly a symptom of lacking a full load in other things. Nevertheless, the reproach has to be risked: names direct us so successfully to the very site of our discontent because discontent keeps us busy. The harmlessness of this name "keeping oneself busy" will not make a career for itself.

People thought that with the "will to power" what primarily matters after the epochs of raw violence is now or very soon "the power to define." The one who exercises this power determines the concepts with which reality is processed and used. But the expression "the power to define" demands or assumes a measure of precision that approaches the target value [*Sollwert*] of the legislator's work. The power given to humanity in paradise was the power to name, not to define. What mattered was to call the lion and that it came, and not to know what it was when it didn't come. Whoever can call things by their names doesn't need to comprehend them. The strength of names has thereby remained greater in magic than in every type of comprehending. The tyranny of names is grounded in names having maintained an air of magic: to promise contact with what hasn't been comprehended.

Rescue Without Sinking

I don't want uninterrupted exertions undertaken for my rescue if I don't know that I am in danger.

There are too many people who think they have found their meaning in life by rescuing others; they therefore do not shy away from talking others into believing that they are lost.

I see these people on the street and on television, in the newspapers and in books, at the lectern and at the pulpit—with every new medium in full force—ready for and almost taking action for my rescue. I see that they don't care at all about whether I need to be rescued.

This is a *novum* in history: Never have so many people become active for the sake of others without being asked to do so.

Fundamental Differences

Foundation and Soil, Bottom and Ground: Hitting Bottom, Getting to the Bottom of Things, Standing on the Ground

One hits bottom [*Grund*] by sinking.[1] One gets to the bottom of things by immersing oneself in them. For the shipwrecked, the bottom of the sea has always been the final stop, which no living person can reach. This was, indeed, an ultimate foundation [*Letztbegründung*], but in the ironic sense that from here one could neither start out nor rise up in a founding manner to what was founded.

The reason [*Grund*] for a thing didn't always have to be an ultimate one: only *one* reason for *one* thing and not the one reason for all things, beginning with water and all the way to the Being of beings. It is a humble claim to want to get to the bottom of a thing; it only means that one isn't satisfied with its surface. *The* foundation [*Grund*] of things is admittedly *one* even without all metaphysics and entirely within the limits of its own metaphorics. The bottom of the ocean is ultimately the same surface of the earth that rises out of the depths along the shores and becomes for all human undertakings the foundation of life, farmland, the land for paths, and the building site [*Lebensgrund, Ackerboden, Wegeland und Baugrund*]. It is only *one* foundation that lets one hit bottom just as it bears and nourishes and lets live. Or it deceptively presents itself as between these two, between this and that as moor and swamp for sinking without a trace as well as for the path-seeking use of small payloads.

The unity of reason [*Grund*] has near-to-life vividness even before it becomes a conceptual allure for metaphysical speculation and transcendental absolutisms. To have the ultimate foundation and thereby to possess security for everything that needs founding is the epitome of reason's

---

1. Throughout this section, "Fundamental Differences," Blumenberg explores and plays on the metaphoric field opened up in the difference between *Grund* and *Boden*. Unfortunately, neither of these German terms can be translated in a simple, unique way into English. According to context, *Grund* will be translated as "bottom," "foundation," "reason," or even "site" (in the case of *Baugrund*, "building site"), while *Boden* will be rendered as "soil," "ground," or "land."—Trans.

achievements and, so it appears, is far removed from mere metaphorics. This is also the pride of the critique of reason, although never an entirely convincing one. Talk about reason [*Grund*]—even about the "essence of reason [*Wesen des Grundes*]"—is saturated with imagination, which gladly pretends to be language's forerunner for the understanding of Being.

The metaphorics of soil [*Boden*] (in which everything that grows and bears fruit and nourishes takes root) *and* the metaphorics of foundation [*Grund*] (upon which everything durable and solid works and stands, is built and erected) do not seem to be easily brought together in imagination: roots require the soil's porousness and permeability to allow trees and plants to rise to the light from which they first properly take life; on the other hand, a human building demands rocklike density and insolubility for the foundation it rests upon. These "fundamental differences" of the ground of life [*"Grundverschiedenheiten" des Lebensboden*] also seem to condition divergent worldviews and lifestyles: the cultivating and the constructing. At any time, one's gaze checks the soil for opposing properties, a process that extends into the reciprocal metaphorics with which these properties offer themselves up for understanding. The letting-grow of the "culture of the soil" calls for the plow and the harrow, for slicing and plowing through the untouched sterile surface; the will to construct aims for smoothing and stabilizing, for load capacity and surface load, wants nothing from the depths and does everything against the depths. At the same time, everything that is erected upon and lasts through the bearing foundation will optically deny this base. Scarcely having been laid, foundations disappear beneath the concealed nature of their function; one only exposes them when the structure starts to crack. Optically, every construct repudiates the imposition that something else could ever stand or thrive in its place or in any way be disposed to the primary ambivalence of the soil. This is what disturbs the view of a landscape, where what grows is interspersed with or even displaced by what has been built [*Gegründeten*]. Here nothing appears to be able to grow again, just like on those old paths that haven't been traveled or walked upon for a long time.

In the duality of these perspectives and lifestyles, there slumbers a dualism that can burst into raw hostility at any time. Cain was hostile to Abel because the one with the first sacrifice from his herd appeared to have won God's favor by supposedly sparing the soil through a nomadic lifestyle, while Cain's fruits of farming had been rejected as an exploitation of the injured soil in the sight of the God of the nomads—a memory of the Garden Paradise and a transferring of the curse of being expelled from it.

It may be that man's longing is again and again directed at overcoming the hidden or open enmity between lifestyles. The trust in the solidity of the ground [*Boden*] should be connected to rootedness in it as a metaphor for settledness, fidelity, family bonds, the order of inheritance, which one can cultivate and build for generations on end. The fact that this ideal can be dangerous is shared with other ideals of harmonizing incompatible things. The more difficult it is to make things compatible and to unite them, the more the determination to do so can work itself up into a cult that—like all cults—wants its victims and priests.

Back when one still had no idea about the kind of disastrous energies that could be contained in the cult of the soil, the figure of phlegmatic settledness was an exotic theatrical pleasure recalling distant Rousseauism: the equally simple and dull life as an atavistic shudder of big city aesthetics. In 1908, the dramatist Karl Schönherr brought his comedy of elementary life bearing the powerful name *Erde* [*Earth*] before the eyes and souls of the city-dwellers. The critic Alfred Polgar saw onstage exactly the coincidence of "fundamental differences," of bearing-foundation and rooting-foundation [*Traggrund und Wurzelgrund*]: "With heavy steps, Schönherr's farmers traverse their soil almost as if they haven't been freed very long from the plantlike condition of being firmly rooted." Concerning the main figure, the old farmer Grutz, the critic says that he is a "favored son of mother earth" and nothing less than "the personified primordial power of the soil." For this reason, he may and must rise up one more time from his deathbed (where he already lies) and procreate [*fortpflanzen*] a last time—whereby only listening to the word "procreate" almost a century later astoundingly draws attention to the fact that humans, too, when they most urgently stand under the sway of nature and enjoy being more animalistic than any animal, have something plantlike [*Pflanzenhaftes*] according to the unerring sense of language.

Back in spring of the year 1908, Josef Kainz played the old farmer Grutz. Alfred Polgar praised him according to all the rules of the art of criticism. But after he finishes praising him, Polgar has a sentence ready that cunningly consists of two half sentences: "That was splendid; but: where was the farmer?" Apart from the costume and dialect, Kainz could have just as well been a king, a slaveholder, or a big industrialist. According to Polgar, one ought to have been able to "sense immediately" the identity of the earth and the farmer "and not just hear about it."

Who knows whether Polgar clung all his life [1873–1955] to this concept of "identity" and the desire for its immediate perceptibility? Wasn't it precisely the objectionable changeability of Josef Kainz's habits, hinting at an immanent "fundamental difference" independent of the intentions of the play and its actors, that one thought one was dealing with theatrically, never suspecting the dislocations that a quarter of a century later would shake the ground, which here as *Earth* amazed an audience that knew nothing of what was to come?

Standing and Constancy

There is an anthropological aspect to the metaphorics of ground. The two-legged human stands on the ground in a manner that is so peculiar to it that this standing is not a standing position [*Stand*] in the sense of constancy [*Bestand*] or a condition [*Zustand*] but rather is an activity. It is not language that leads us to believe this; rather, language follows the discovery that one has to do this in order to not *not* do it [*um es nicht zu lassen*].

A stone lies on the ground; as long as other forces don't act on it, the stone complies with the principle of inertia and with the gravity constantly effecting it. The vase stands on the table as long as the table can support it and no one takes the vase away. It can be said that the table has properties that enable it to support the vase on it. The vase is a burden for the table, but this is not one of its real predicates. Standing is not an activity for [inanimate] physical bodies. A human being who stands on the ground at a particular place acts out, in a strict sense, a complex operation that can be physiologically demonstrated. His relation to the ground is in this respect real, although objectively the ground is only the surface of a heavenly body, and the one standing on it has no real relation to the heavenly body. He is not there for this body, and this body isn't there for him.

The fact that standing on the ground is an activity, indeed, an exertion, is shown through an organism's potential fatigue in achieving it, as well as through the consequences of this fatigue. What he executes is not merely the principle of inertia. He is not held by gravity, since gravity is what constantly demands that he undertake measures to even out the instability of his balance. If one were to hinder the person standing from such regulative procedures, he would fall over and come to the ground in the "situation [*Lage*]" of the stone.

To stand is to not fall over. Standing demands a certain minimum of watchful attention; it doesn't permit the frivolousness of limitlessly letting-oneself-go (as it is not accidentally called), of letting-oneself-fall in resignation. To be sure, one falls on the same ground that one had been standing on. The ground one stands on *can* only be the one that one falls on. For there is only one ground—only in agriculture does one speak of different types of ground [*Böden*] with different qualities and degrees of suitability; the planet has and bestows only one.

The Building Site

The notion that the modern era has turned humanity's gaze and desire from the heavens to the earth and brought them from transcendence back to immanence is a commonplace characterized by a bit of inaccuracy. Comparing the *summae* of the medieval Scholastics with the cathedrals of the time, one thinks of both architectural skill and the rising vertical tendency, from the lifting up of one's heart to the speculative proof of God's existence. The notion that this vertical direction also contained the losing of oneself found in mysticism, in enthusiastic rapture, in the pleasure in the unfathomable, and in humility in the face of God's hiddenness, had to arouse and form the resistance that led to the beginnings of the modern era. Yet comparisons that are supposed to help in applying the unity of a signature to an age can easily seduce. Thus, the structure of the gothic cathedral was also a phenomenon of limitation vis-à-vis the heights that rendered perceptible matter's finitude in the face of the brightness of the heavens. To have sought out this contour against the heights unites the scholastic way of thinking as a constructive force even more with the cathedral. One easily forgets that the criticism of the most magnificent proof of God's existence, Anselm of Canterbury's "ontological proof," had already been victorious in the Middle Ages, while at the height of German idealism sympathy for the effort to prove existence from concepts alone arose once again. The difference of epochs can, however, be illustrated by architectural structures. Not only because the gaze now sinks toward the earth; it is also directed purposefully and in a concentrated way to the question of foundations instead of toward vaults and tracery, tower and peaks. The building site [*Baugrund*] determines whether something can be built at all, what can be built and how. The insistence on testing foundation and soil, on testing the ability to be grounded [*Gründbarkeit*] and load-bearing capacity characterizes the theoretical "thoroughness [*Gründlichkeit*]" of the modern era. Many "systems" seem constructed only for demonstrating what the ground could bear and how solidly the foundation had been laid. Due to this kind of absolute thoroughness, such systems almost never came to the metaphorical completion of building—and for this reason it has never surrendered its entirely peculiar power to impress.

Descartes imagines that the science made possible by his *Discourse on Method* follows the model of rational urban planning. The draft of a whole can only be kept without deterrence and deviation, if one takes everything that had previously been built—the unplanned growth and winding use of space as predetermined by walls and moats in medieval cities—and literally levels it to the ground and, thus, renders the ground capable of being developed according to rules. Only by visualizing the *Method* is the all-too-limited *fundamentum inconcussum* of the "I think" extended in space, which against all doubt provides its weight-bearing capacity with the degree of its capacity to be settled—its metaphorical "habitability." Descartes himself may have recalled cases in which the burning of a city enabled a regulated new construction; one thinks of Poitiers as his model. In the Cartesian century, planned cities were called *villes à la Descartes*. The fundamental idea was: everything depended on constructing an entire science as if it had been realized by a single person—just as buildings designed by a single architect were more perfect than those of several architects, especially if they reused preexisting brickwork (*en faisant servir de vieilles murailles qui avaient été bâties à d'autres fins*). Even if one cannot envisage tearing down all of a city's houses to build them entirely anew, Descartes writes, there are still many people who tear down an old house to build it anew when its foundation isn't entirely secure— here one doesn't wait for its collapse or a fire.

This extensive metaphorics describes the beginning epoch's "care" for its foundations, especially with regard to everything passed on to it as tradition. This epoch arose not only through doubt and uncertainty about this tradition; as an unknown factor, there was also immediately the unforeseeable nature of the new, which the building site always has to bear. With respect to the accumulated discoveries and their "solidity," the recourse to the foundations and their testing became more difficult, and annoyance about admonitions regarding ascertainment increased. Finally, in the face of the pride of those having something built for themselves, the dramatists of foundations would isolate themselves at the topping-off ceremony. Those who had already fallen in line with the unavoidable nature of empirical mass success contemptuously called one of the last attempts at constructing optimized powers of comprehension "pyramidism." In 1929, Wilhelm Ostwald gave the title *Die Pyramide der Wissenschaften* [*The Pyramid of the Sciences*] to what he used to oppose the resigned form of a merely two-dimensional "combination" of insights into nets as especially represented by the Vienna Circle. The metaphor of "nets [*Netze*]," which was still far removed from the pinnacle of its success, could however help us imagine one thing metaphorically: nets require a medium and no longer a ground [*Boden*].

At the same time, Moritz Schlick, the founder of the Vienna Circle, certainly saw the development of the metaphorics of mesh, narrow or wide, with distrust. A 1934 treatise of his bearing the defiant title *Über das Fundament der Erkenntnis* [*On the Foundation of Knowledge*] laments the rampantly waning consideration of foundational requirements [*Gründungserfordernisse*], commending those who "search for the rock that is there before all building takes place and that doesn't sway." For just this reason the "physicalism" fostered in Cambridge, Warsaw, Berlin, and Vienna did not suffice for him; the reassurance that all sciences could be connected by physics and its language was rash. The fact that one could use the stigma "metaphysics" to bring into disrepute principles that didn't satisfy the criterion of connectability and were thus called "isolated principles" reveals how the "solid ground of absolute certainty" had been relinquished. For Schlick, this would be a concession that could only coincide with the end of philosophy itself, which he was neither prepared for nor desired.

But in June 1936, Moritz Schlick was murdered in Vienna. This was certainly not desirable for the people inclined toward great renunciations of foundations and architectonics; but it relieved its programmatic supporters [*Programmatiker*] from considering someone who still had believed in a rock-solid ground to be built on, at least one who held this demand (even while mistrustful of its ability to be fulfilled) as the indispensable stigma of the philosopher. Otto Neurath saw the model of theoretical unity emerging from the postulate of connection and proceeding up to the renewal of the idea of an "encyclopedia." He opposed the influence of Wittgenstein, whose *Tractatus* served as the basis for the Vienna Circle's concept formation, by using the always available reproach of metaphysical tendencies. But he also countered the empirical theoreticians of verification and falsification with his own metaphors, which renounced fantasies of finality and spoke instead of "probation and tremors." More than the first term, the second betrays that at stake was an instability of the ground, which was no longer tied to the problem of the building site. As so often, one believed that one could erase the traces of absolutism with a linguistic coup: his starting point had been the promise of emancipation from absolutism. The condition of Archimedes, which had understandably already appeared to Neurath as unrealizable, also meant the theoretically unattainable: "We do not have a stable point from which we could turn the earth upside down: and, in the same way, we have no absolutely solid ground upon which we could erect the sciences." Neurath had already invented the new metaphor of the threat of an earthquake in 1932 against the "protocol statements" that Rudolph Carnap had offered, full of hope. The fiction of constructing an "ideal language" with such sentences seemed to Neurath to be once again "metaphysical"—and this no less than the imaginary figure introduced by Laplace of an intelligence covering the universe in its totality.

It was a reversion from Descartes's dream of unshakable stabilization to Heraclitus's flowing universe. At the IX International Congress of Philosophy in Paris in 1937, Neurath deduced: "We have no absolute foundation from which we can proceed. . . . Science in all its aspects is always under discussion. Everything flows."

Farmland

"Behind the plowshare walks the sower." Who said this? I would always answer right away: the late Heidegger. But he also read the one to whom it belonged. Nietzsche wrote it during his year in Sorrento [1876–77] in a notebook preparing the never completed *Untimely Meditation* that initially bore the title *We Philologists* and then became a collection of aphorisms called *The Plowshare*, only to be ultimately subsumed into *Human, All Too Human.*

We can no longer view this image without the uneasiness radiating from country idylls that awaken the impression of the irreversible nature of fundamental forms of life. Through countless preparations of attentiveness, one's gaze is directed entirely at the sower: at the calm hand disseminating the seed, at his incomprehensible trust in the seed's growth, at his annoying certainty of not being able to be ruined together with fruit and harvest despite the threatening weather images from satellites. Those who are forced to grant this image of the sower are comrades from another time, as if from another star, who consider and perform their procreation with mistrust and who see disaster coming from the ruthlessness with which nature does its thing. For the spirit of these times, sowers behind plowshares appear as functionaries of a gloomy reproduction agency that lets meaninglessness run rampant in the realm of the always-the-same. Nietzsche's farmer arouses suspicion, because he could stand as an emblem for every agenda: a figure of trust, of solid as well as frivolous trust.

The gaze directed in such a way fails to notice that it is precisely Nietzsche who uses the motto—and rarely uses something in a way that everyone would expect from him. Taken in this way, it is immediately apparent that the sharpness of the plowshare is much more important to him than the sower walking behind it. A different text from the same context expresses it clearly enough: "The plowshare cuts into the hard and the soft soil; it passes over highs and lows and draws it close to itself." In "Schopenhauer as Educator" [*Untimely Meditation* III], Nietzsche had already found the unsurpassable formulation: "There will be no deeper furrows than those that his plowshare will tear in the ground of recent humanity." Indeed, the plow turns the ground into farmland [*Acker*], but that is not what captivates the gaze of one watching this tearing up of what is untouched or worn down. Before the ground becomes something else, it is what we stand and walk on, set up and sit on, build and found on—the unnoticed reliability of what is self-evident.

Only when it is injured, when it is tossed or piled up, is it apparent that the ground has depth, and that penetrating what is uncut and untorn produces a new visibility that no longer seems to be defined by standing and walking, placing and laying—that its depths await something else, something that it is only here and now decided will be a sower. There was nothing accidental about the straightforward word order of Nietzsche's sentence.

The Swamp

With every thinker one finds metaphors that seem to belong more to the epoch than to him. Occasionally, they expose the background of the thinker's technical questions and technical decisions. By moving him into a horizon of his contemporaries—perhaps by showing him as subjected to a Zeitgeist—metaphors, however, remain informative by displacements and disfigurations that can still be added to them and that let the force of a particular individual be grasped vis-à-vis the universal.

But there are also metaphors that appear to only personally befit their author. More than anything else, the accuracy of such metaphors collects into an image what otherwise could only be derived diffusely and presumably from complete works. They stand as if in the center of a horizon and illustrate the uniqueness of the relation between a person and a situation. It remains a stroke of luck to find such metaphors and to pause before them, hesitating the way one hesitates at the mere inkling of a significant revelation. Familiarity with the work alone is not sufficient for this. It could be something like a phenomenological act that splays itself out in moments and, against the rules, on the level of the singular.

Every thorough reader of Wittgenstein one day encounters the metaphor of a swamp bounded by a wall. Swamp and wall—where would one ever find these two elements juxtaposed? For the wall cannot be identical with the border of the swamp. The wall forms the circumference of the swamp and encloses it, but stands, however—as is required of walls—upon a solid foundation. In the *Philosophische Bemerkungen* [*Philosophical Remarks*] completed in publishable form by its preface in 1930, Wittgenstein writes that the wall is "a sign for the fact that within its realm there is a swamp, but not that the swamp is just as big as the area that is bordered by the wall."

The image needs no explanation. It shows that there are transitions that do not allow definite boundaries. It is evident with the colors of the spectrum that orange, on the one side, borders on red as red-orange, but on the other side, as yellow-orange, borders on yellow. Yet this evidence doesn't allow us to come to the opposite conclusion that absolute orange necessarily lies exactly at the midpoint between the two borders. It doesn't only *have* transitions, it *is* a transition. Another example Wittgenstein uses is the vibrating hundred-sided polygon that turns into a circle. Here as elsewhere, exact demarcation of inexactness is impossible.

The border of the swamp must run between the swamp and the solid building site on which the wall enclosing the swamp can be built. But this border matters little. Only what is within the wall and securely enclosed by it is not insignificant. Everything depends on no one ending up in the swamp; nothing depends on the wall exactly marking the border of the swamp. The wall's function is screening off, not announcing. It has to stand where one can be sure either that one has not yet reached the swamp—or that one knows it is definitely behind one.

Wittgenstein's metaphor also has the formal rank that befits its informative value for his way of thinking. It has the degree of precision that his images and analogies always assume when he speaks of imprecision.

I support this by pointing out its difference from a rather helpless, unspecific, and entirely impersonal use of the swamp metaphor by Edmund Husserl. He wrote it down to illustrate the mental situation of his philosophical early days in the German city Halle: "In philosophical work, I decided to renounce all great goals and to be happy if, in the swamps of an insupportable lack of clarity, I could work out only here and there the smallest solid ground for myself. Thus, I continued on from despair to despair, from picking myself up to picking myself up." There is no imprecision here. No matter how small the piece of solid ground may be that Husserl uses to promise himself the happiness of surmounted uncertainty, it only has to bear this one person who is almost lost, and does bear him, until he must continue on. With great constancy, it is not the metaphor of borders but rather of the saving, load-bearing ground that would be significant for Husserl's phenomenology, which at the time still lay far in the future.

With Wittgenstein, one could forget that the swamp was a phrase of the epoch, but not with Husserl. Goethe's blind Faust raised the enmity between swamp and human work to the signature of intolerance toward the given: "A swamp runs along the hills / Infesting all that has been achieved; / To drain the rotten, foul pool / Would be the greatest achievement [Ein Sumpf zieht am Gebirge hin, / Verpestet alles schon Errungene; / Den faulen Pfuhl auch abzuziehen, / Das letzte wär das Höchsterrungene]." This is anything but a metaphor with a philosophical aim, but contrary to its author's intention, it hypostasizes itself into one.

Only a year after Wittgenstein wrote his *Philosophical Remarks*, Otto Neurath, the programmatic head of the Viennese Circle, drafted *Empiricism and Sociology*, paying tribute to the Zeitgeist by diversely distributing word-combinations with "life" throughout the text—like that of a "life-ground," upon which the totality of "life-conditions" condition the "life-situation" and, as an end-result, the "life-mood." This complex presupposes what Neurath formulates in a single sentence, as if taking leave of the insoluble aspects of the epoch: "Humanity becomes more and more independent of the ground it lives on." As proof he offers the drastic turn that the relation between swamp and life has finally taken: "When a human and a swamp used to come together, the human disappeared. Now it's the swamp."

From the perspective of this triumphant position, what Wittgenstein had imagined a year earlier appears to be the worldwide, unbridgeable difference of a worry [*Sorge*] that no progress could remedy.

The antinomy of these almost simultaneous metaphors betrays more about the fault lines ready to burst in the temporal structure than the analytic efforts working on the mental situation of the times would be capable of.

"Asphalt" and "Swamp"—A Dualism

In 1934, in the August volume of the journal *Die Sammlung* [The Collection] edited by Klaus Mann, Bertolt Brecht published an article for the fiftieth birthday of Lion Feuchtwanger with the title "Asphalt Literature."

Using the deadly word from Goebbels's slobbering against the intelligentsia of the Weimar Republic as the inscription of a gift to a friend was designed not only to provoke. It was also one of the rhetorical tricks that, despite its risks, dares again and again to deprive the enemy of its own language. The ultimate goal: to render the enemy speechless by turning its means against it. It was 1934, and resignation in the face of the unscrupulous *Apparat* of vile fabrications spun by the Nazi "Ministry of People's Enlightenment [*Volksaufklärung*] and Propaganda" had not yet come into its own.

Brecht performs his linguistic reversal in a single sentence of metaphoric antinomy: "Only the swamp brings charges against his big brother, the asphalt: the patient, clean, and useful brother." If one were not a half-century further along, one would pause at such pleasure in the *coup de parole*. The change of times doesn't sanction this favor.

The change of times forces the reflection of whether it is still possible after half a century to make use of this means of resistance. It doesn't require much pondering to arrive at "no," to establish the obsolescence of this lightning-like triumph.

In welding intellectuals and literati to asphalt, Goebbels had counted on the aversions to big cities in wide segments of the population: the asphalting of streets and lanes, one of the 1920s' most visually conspicuous encouragements to further traffic, had changed the image of cities and villages hitherto shaped by road surfaces patterned in granite and basalt. Producing sterile, smooth surfaces and sealing off the ground was the odious means to quicker road construction, less street noise, and easier work procedures. The asphalt Jew [*Asphaltjude*], Goebbels meant to suggest, belonged to this world of all-encompassing monotony and sterility, in which green no longer grew in the cracks between age-old cobblestones. The subversion of the vitality of the "folk," the slinking poison undermining it, was supposedly thus enabled to move smoothly and silently.

Brecht lets the swamp do the defaming of the patience, cleanliness, and usefulness of the asphalt. This speechifier could not know that swamps would have a great future as inaccessible refuges for living things. That importunate humans might sink in them was only one of nature's protective measures and a mark of the ungainliness of an oppressor growing weary of self. Sympathizers would flee in droves from the swamps to the asphalt, the somewhat more brittle brother of the concrete that makes it less than omnipresent, competing with it to finally smother the living ground with meaningless surface smoothness and foil any hope of a rampant return.

In the long run, Brecht's metaphorical dualism had no chance. The swamps weren't growing but shrinking. That brought sympathy to their side in a fury. Sympathy and fury had never been on the side of asphalt; in this respect, even in 1934, Goebbels was not to be outmaneuvered by touting the advantages of covering everything with petroleum derivatives, something that would soon enough again be denounced as of secondary importance in the syndrome of constant achievement.

One sees here a disturbingly constant and sentimental affectability [*Affizierbarkeit*]. The malicious or, rather, maleficent virtuoso trimmer of a people's soul had placed his bets on an enduring fundamental mood, knowing full well that its apparent good nature concealed a proper willing capacity to recognize the enemy, which created, in turn, the appearance of pest controllers and decontaminators—the bloody pathos of cultural therapy [*Kulturtherapie*]—for a burgeoning cohort of murderous accomplices.

One doesn't have to wait spellbound for the return of identical metaphors to receive confirmation of the lurking disposition, to see it step out of its hiding places. In the background lies a dualism that withdraws itself in metamorphoses, at times called the dualism of nature and culture, then culture and civilization. Although it is thoroughly satisfied that only one side, the antipodal, is named in a verbally destructive way, the other local side remains undefined and open for sympathetic appropriation by anyone who stakes his soul against "the" spirit, his community against "the" society, his self-determination against "the" power," in short: "his" Everything against "the" Nothingness. What one *sees*—from the distance necessary for every perspective—is always already the negation of the proper, of what is one's own. No one gladly adds for oneself: how could it be any different?

Beneath the Foundations

The solidity of the building site [*Baugrund*] is a privileged metaphor of modernity. As soon as one no longer perceives the *Sursum corda*! [Lift up your hearts!], one lowers one's gaze toward what has to bear everything else as opposed to what strives away from it.

It may be that there are older images for what foundations have to achieve: they not only lie on top of the building site, they also cover what may already have existed and been built beneath them. The banal explanation for this fact—that is, one builds again and again in the same place upon what already exists because in this manner one can reuse a maintained, stabilized foundation with the most available materials—is plausible but not enough. As Christian constructions upon pagan substrata reveal, it is also a matter of the ostensible triumph: none of the gods stirred to defend what had been built to honor and to nourish them. The cultic *damnatio memoriae* simultaneously shows and makes disappear.

That is not all. The covering up of the old with the new, the embedding of the conquered in the foundations of its conqueror has an apotropaic, exorcising, assuring function: whatever has had to put up with such treatment cannot come back into existence. It is the production of the determinant "past."

It is dubious whether the metaphor of the nurturing soil intervenes and encroaches here as well: the fundamental idea of the humus-rich fertility of the cultivated foundation [*Grund*] saturated with sediments of culture. On April 20, 1938, in the old Acropolis Museum in Athens, Ernst Jünger seized on an idea for his diary inspired by cult objects in the shapes of snakes and bulls excavated from beneath the "Persian rubble"—"Tellurian beings" rather than Olympic ones—that had been buried in the ground when the new temple was built [in the fifth century BCE]: "It is a great law: the evidence of earlier cults is always concealed beneath the foundations of great sanctuaries; the new, loftier veneration sinks its roots into the humus of the old one." Beneath the palladia and altars, Jünger notes, there are graves, crypts, and catacombs. "In a mysterious way, they play a part in the sacrifice, like the Old Testament in the New."

If one heeds the extent to which the Old Testament burdened and almost rendered impossible the acceptance and consistency of the New Testament during the great Gnostic crisis, it is not the Christianization of the issue in the argument's final intensification that is dubious. Rather, if one thinks of Pauline justification, the dubiousness lies much more in superposing despair in the law—regardless of which form Pharisean pedantry takes in its willingness to fulfill it—as the law's secretive collaboration in mercy. The historical ground as the nurturing humus of whatever formation comes next—this is an all-too-handy, all-too-careless allowance for all the downfalls that the new has prepared for the old. The end of human sacrifice as an insurrection of bloody cults everywhere by God's great sign in demanding *and* preventing Abraham's sacrifice is not the beautiful blossom that grew forth from the decomposition of sacrificial corpses from time immemorial; rather, it is the monument to a magnificent refusal that used a myth to at once trick and sanction the agreement of an angry God and the silencing of an orthodoxy that is always ready to pounce. The ram as a substitute sacrifice had always been accepted, until a new symbolic substitute ended animal sacrifice in the Jerusalem Temple, although a meal of remembrance was still consecrated with the "realism" of flesh and blood.

Similarly, with the sinking of the old generations of Tellurian gods beneath the new temples of the Olympians, it is less a matter of their mysterious continued sway than of their abandonment. The "mystery" does not lie in nourishing soil, but rather in being allowed to forget monstrous horrors. In short, it lies in being allowed to forget the terror of the gods in favor of soliciting their affableness through cults and temples. Just as myth narrates which monstrosities have been overcome and which have been forever exorcised, the insertion of the old idols into the new foundations combines being allowed to forget with the easing memory of what has been sunk. Nothing grows forth or upward from it; everything lies upon and over it in order to use weight and cunning to fight against it rising up. The splendor of temples and the art of their divine images do not tolerate the thought of "roots" that could still extract something nourishing from the "humus." This is precisely the exclusion that is supposed to find its limit in building upon buildings, in making images upon images.

Archeology, which digs in the rubble beneath foundations and brings things to light, is beyond such apotropaic relations: the same museum houses both the Tellurian and the Olympian, snakes and bulls and Zeus and Athena. For people who haven't stopped sealing their own horrors beneath their foundations.

Terra Inviolata

I

From time immemorial, the exegetic people has gazed with awkward confusion at the Bible's primordial history of the first pair of brothers: God graciously accepts the first sacrifice of the cattle breeder Abel, but refuses the fruits of the field from the farmer Cain—all without the sacred text containing a divine commandment or prohibition regarding how humanity should obtain culture and nourishment, according to which the one brother would have acted properly and the other not. The lovers of the unfathomable depths of the will of the divinity (who thus deserved to be called *deus absconditus*) have seen the expression of the will of this "concealed God" in the notion that He selects and rejects as He sees fit.

The ethnological explanation didn't lie too far away: a nomadic people had legitimated in a document the divine pleasure in its way of living and its products and cursed the agriculture of the surrounding pagan peoples, especially the previous slave lords in Egypt. Is this explanation sufficient? One doubts it if already in the Christian era's free-lance apocalyptic literature something returns as a symmetrical promise for the end of time that, as the justification for the first murder in human history, had remained the image of an ungraspable divine decision: Cain's state of being rejected as the consequence of the rejection of his sacrifice.

In the Sibylline Oracles, which continue the sibylline tradition in a Christian manner, one finds the following in hexameter verse, as is fitting for the ecstatically singing sibyl: "Then HE will produce pure convictions / Among humanity, renew the human race. / One will no longer loosen up the earth clod in the depths with crooked plow; / No longer will the bulls plow with straightened iron. [Dann wird ER reine Gesinnung / Unter den Menschen erzeugen, erneuern das Menschengeschlecht. / Nicht mehr wird man die Scholl' in der Tiefe auflockern mit Krummpflug; / Nicht mehr pflügen die Stiere mit gradegerichtetem Eisen]." As a vision of the gentleness of the end of time, this verse couples a change of conviction and a renunciation of culture that looks like an incorporation of Lucretian cultural critique in the Apocalypse, like a divine enforcement of the principle of *terra inviolata*.

In the final realm of "pure conviction"—and it remains enigmatic as to why God was not yet able to give it to Adam, his "image and likeness"— what the earth gives is taken away from it. According to the basic idea of all critique of civilization [*Kulturkritik*], there will be and has to be enough, as long as one doesn't want abundance that is torn from the injured earth with crooked and straight plows. The sibyl may have in mind that the number of those belonging to this holy state and spared the fire will be small enough for her promise of a new culture of gatherers to prove to be true. Is "*Kulturkritik*" supposed to have been one of the motives for condemning the *massa damnata* to eternal ruin? The sibyl's disaster songs are terrible enough!

II

In Hans Freyer's *Theorie des gegenwärtigen Zeitalters* [Theory of the Present Age] (1955), the concept of "secondary system" plays a central role. What is conspicuous is that the necessary correlate to a "secondary system"—namely, the "primary system"—does not once appear as an explicit term in the entire text, but is always presupposed in the imaginatively produced accompanying representations.

In this connection, numerous additional metaphors come into play that circle around the difference between fertility and sterility as the fundamental determinations of both systems. There is no "primary system" because the primary element that offers itself in metaphors cannot have the quality—or, more precisely, the lack of quality—of a "system" that already belongs to the secondary. Between the two realities there exists a relation of irreversibility. This relation has its own metaphors of dismantling and using up, of shoddy mismanagement of capital, of loans, of exhausting reserves. All this explains the schema of both systems, makes it understandable, but also simultaneously lends it a type of superficial evidentiary nature: the organic element, the sturdy administrating element, the primary element, the stratigraphic founding element—all these have suggestive argumentative advantages that are well known and are concentrated in the formula *terra inviolata.*

All this would be less interesting if the author didn't expressly warn about the dangers of this realm of images and show himself to be very familiar with them. He declares himself to be aware that "sociology must exercise the most extreme care when using images taken from organic life. In particular, it is extremely dangerous to characterize the elements of historicity and the continuing effect of inheritance using such images. One reconceives the temporal as spatial, and processes as organic structures." Cultures and civilizations, he says, did not arise by growth but rather by achievement, and there are beginnings to decisions in history that have no complete parallels in the realm of organic life.

Despite having declared himself aware of the danger of such metaphorics, Freyer falls back into his imaginative system of orientation a few lines later. The present age, he writes, is radically serious about the possibility of the "secondary system" and has reached the point of an impossible reversal. This modern system, he continues, is to be characterized as an entire and complete world or, rather, is about to become such a world. "The attempt to pour a concrete foundation and to build a structure in a 'hovering' style upon it has now actually been undertaken, and to the extent it succeeded, the roots would have to have been cut through and the capillaries blocked." The ground [*Boden*], understood as what has grown, is used up in felling trees, turning karstic, and becoming steppe, and the old metaphor of "groundlessness [*Bodenlosigkeit*]"—as artistic carelessness—returns not only in every sense of mismanagement and devastation but also with the intention of exposing the surrogates of the ground. Thus Freyer writes concerning language as a "secondary system" that it is "completely groundless; wanting to slip a ground beneath language would contradict the principle of its cultivation." And the dilemma of modern man in reestablishing the balance of nature's forces that have been disturbed by him is described in the following words: "After he has mismanaged the ground in the actual sense of the word, he attempts to slip a new ground beneath his rational economy." But it is precisely here that the talk of the ground should illustrate the excluded feasibility of what has grown: "Nature has the last word when it is a matter of the equilibrium of nature, of the 'ground' in the actual sense of the word, and nature's answer can arrive via detours and from a completely different corner than was expected."

This brief paradigm serves as a nod toward the need for a "metaphorology" of critiques of civilization [*Kulturkritik*], which have, if not their own jargon, then at least their own imaginative background.

On Board · Transformations of a Metaphor

Georg Simmel dedicated his often reprinted study *Goethe* to Max Weber's wife, Marianne, whose *Lebenserinnerungen* [Memoirs] reproduce the letter, dated December 9, 1912, that Simmel wrote her in response to her thanking him for the dedication. This letter is one of the strangest transformations that the nautical metaphorics for the philosopher's self-understanding has experienced since antiquity.

Simmel writes about how he would like his book to be understood: as an aid to the German people in "realizing the tremendous treasure" that it possesses in Goethe, "almost without knowing it." Even back then, this was an exaggeration. To this day, the reason for this exaggeration lies in its object: Goethe makes anyone who gets involved with him believe that other authors could not possibly have also or already found what appears to be reserved for this one author alone.

Whoever writes about Goethe on the basis of this experience scarcely stands at the beginning of something. For Simmel as well, the book is, as he writes to Frau Weber, a conclusion. But not the conclusion of a lifework—rather, the conclusion of a work phase in this life and with the phase's instruments. Here the gesture of a great self-confidence commences: "I now tack my sail and seek untrodden land." This is a conventional formulation, especially coming from one who knew Nietzsche and his comparisons with Columbus so well. But this nautical maneuver is already retracted in the projected end: "Admittedly, the journey will certainly come to an end before it reaches the coast." Do dreary premonitions press upon Simmel, who only had six years left to live? Scarcely. He provided an image for his scarcely exhausted model of a life philosophy: life offers life no other chance than that of the fragment. Life's contingency shows what the individual and its finitude are all about: a life ends, life goes on—there are no arrivals on the shores of the *terra incognita*. The danger that Simmel now conjures up is the general misrecognition of this situation by those who, with claims to a system, always want a whole.

They are the "comrades" whom he speaks about and whose behavior scares him off and drives him to separate himself from them: comrades who "make themselves at home on the ship so that they ultimately think that the ship itself is the new land."

What Simmel wants to say with the final position he takes in the Goethe book becomes clear to each of his readers, when they have read his book on Rembrandt published four years later. Simmel achieves a new descriptive level, and does so by renouncing (painfully) a proven terminology. A book without any posture of finality. The reader still has to live with the images, not one of which appears in the book. Therefore, the author can let himself fall, surrender, and fail before reaching the untrodden country.

Simmel oriented himself by means of the metaphor of flowing life developed by Bergson. He doesn't put to sea, he doesn't arrive, he only changes the direction of the sail—he has always been on the high seas. Even the origin, the point of departure, has no determinateness. There will be no harbor, but also no island where one could shipwreck before reaching the goal. "Suffering shipwreck [*Scheitern*]"—that is a metaphor for experiencing a limit that will first arrive with the philosophy of existence that follows upon life philosophy. But what is the other option if the ship isn't supposed to become one's homeland? In the letter to Marianne Weber, this remains open. But there is no doubt that Simmel is thinking about death. Death is not something that is intuited or that comes prematurely, but rather the indispensable complement of life philosophy: life can only preserve itself through the death of each of its "delegates," none of whom have a claim to *be* it, only to take part in it—the final *methexis* [participation] in the remnant of all ideas, the end of Platonism in the nonconcept of "life." One has to die on board. This implies neither a longing for death nor a death drive. It is an unwillingness toward every new totality, uneasiness with unities even of the type that Gestalt-theory and the systematics of symbolic forms had to offer or intended to offer. "Life" gives itself form and shape but not without the proviso of taking it back, of melting it down, as if the supply of substance is too meager to be able to leave it at what already exists. As the author of *The Philosophy of Money* knows, death is an economy of life, of the substance that is always and essentially in too short a supply.

Indispensable as an enticement, the "untrodden land" is not trodden upon. To confuse the ship itself with land has remained a temptation, all the more so after the "idealization" of "suffering shipwreck," of "failing [*Scheitern*]." To make oneself at home on the ship doesn't need to be called a false sense of comfortableness or forgetting one's "proper" home-land as origin or destination. It could also mean making the ship the sole "topic," because its seaworthiness demands this and nothing else. The ship becomes the "care," the "concern [*Sorge*]" of the comrades, and it is the life philosopher who makes himself suspicious by being unwilling to participate in it so as to abandon himself to the stream of life and to my-thologize death as an erotic union with "life." The fundamental metaphor of the situation, however, mustn't get lost: one no longer has the choice of going to sea or staying home. Pascal was able to express it so succinctly: "Vous êtes embarqué."

What one calls an "open conclusion" in theoretical aesthetics could not yet be said in Pascal's language. After failing itself failed, after suf-fering shipwreck itself suffered shipwreck [*Scheitern sogar des Scheiterns*], an "open conclusion" has become unquestionable; defined as a "border situation," even such shipwreck was always only a touching upon, not a crossing of the border—how could it have otherwise become a richly articulated "experience"? Even a death that never lets Dasein as a being-toward-death out of its grasp and that comes to the deficient forlornness of the "one" [*Man-Verlorenheit*] only as an "unexpected blow" no longer belongs to the type of external fatality. To be on board always already de-mands new preparations for Dasein's nautical metaphorics.

To never arrive not only taxes the passenger's confidence and the crew's courage and power; it also poses the question of the seaworthiness of the ship. Simmel viewed his contemporary co-thinkers as being in danger of making themselves at home on the ship and mistaking it for the *terra incognita*—he forgot that "care" for the ship doesn't have to be forgetful-ness about the determination of its goal, although it can be. In the wake of the discussion provoked by Wittgenstein's *Tractatus*, there was also a new version of the metaphor of sea travel with an "open conclusion," as doubts about the ability to idealize language now spread to the state of efficiency of science as a whole, its attainable elements of precision and conclusions. In the Vienna Circle—which emerged from discussions about Wittgenstein's early work initiated by Moritz Schlick in 1922 at the Mathematical Institute at the University of Vienna—Rudolph Carnap's postulate of "protocol statements" led to a lively controversy concerning the attainability of a linguistic statement's "fundamentals," into which Otto Neurath introduced a new metaphorics as a rhetorical show piece.

Neurath had already used it in 1921 in his *Anti-Spengler* to lend the older "conceptual net" a new urgency. One could always only work with the entire net of concepts, whose condition at each point affected the function as a whole, so that every change required testing the stability everywhere. A net is a tool; a ship is a vehicle, a location, a ground, something like a "heavenly body." The transition from one casting a net to a sailor is qualitative, because there would not only be "something" to lose or forfeit. Complete substitution remains out of consideration: "We are like sailors who have to rebuild their ship upon the open sea without ever being able to have a fresh start from bottom up." There is no ideal language that first has to be constructed, because language always already presupposes expanding and correcting—in language, with language—its capacity to satisfy the circumstances: "Wherever one beam is removed another one must immediately take its place, and during this the rest of the ship is used as support. In this way, the ship can be completely refashioned with the help of old beams and driftwood—but only by gradually rebuilding." Once on board, once out to sea, the sailor is assigned to the boat in a more radical way than anyone else is to a vehicle; the metaphor "It's easy to handle [es liege ihm gut in der Hand]" is rather apotropaic. One can no longer handle and work on [*Hand anlegen*] this thing [the boat] as need be: one's standing and hand [*Stand und Hand*] refer to one and the same thing.

Neurath's addition that the ship will ultimately be rebuilt, not only by reusing materials taken from it, from "old beams," but also with "driftwood" contains a small riddle. As soon as one is drawn into the pictorial field [*Bildfeld*], one can scarcely avoid the question of where the driftwood comes from—and the answer is close at hand: other ships were not successful in being repaired at sea, and their shipwreck and sinking is the condition of possibility for carrying out and even expanding the rebuilding of the ship with foreign contributions. The question concerning the "best components" can always only be posed from time to time, from washing up to washing up. In the polemic against Carnap's ideal language, Neurath parades out this aspect.

The fiction of reducing all statements to "protocol statements" and of constructing an ideal language from these statements appears to Neurath—using the most discriminating epithet at his command—as "metaphysical." No less metaphysical than the fiction of universal intelligence introduced by Laplace as an ideal of the exact knowledge of nature, an intelligence that is supposed to be able to derive from *one* world condition any other one. Neurath argues against Carnap—that is, "within the Circle"—that there is no means for constructing sciences from "protocol statements" that have been conclusively cleansed and secured. For this, Neurath continues, an empirical tabula rasa is lacking precisely at the starting point. A decade after launching his *Anti-Spengler*, the unattainable point of departure is illustrated by the analogy of rebuilding a ship: "We are like sailors who have to rebuild their ship upon the open sea without ever being able to take it apart in a dock and reconstruct it from the best components." What Carnap had called "the language of physics as the universal language of science" must be called in metaphor the illusion of building the ship anew on the high seas, for "our historical, trivial language" is always given in advance; in such trivial language, the most annoying "metaphysical" defects can at best be repaired with a "list of prohibited words" in order to arrive at a unified language full of compromises, at a scientific "slang." Neurath came out with various samples of an *Index verborum prohibitorum*—or, better still, exposed himself with this.

If a shudder accompanies the thought of a ship having been repaired and de-metaphysicalized at sea according to Neurath's procedure, then his illustration of the elementary situation has at least contributed to dismantling risky excessive demands. After Laplace's daemon, he used his most powerful metaphor in 1937 to oppose the Archimedean perspective: "We have no stable point from which we could turn the earth upside down; and in the same way we have no absolutely solid ground upon which we could erect the sciences. Our actual situation is as if we were on board a ship on the open sea, and it were necessary to replace different parts of the ship during the journey."

A year before his death in 1945, Neurath ended his last big publication, *Foundations of the Social Sciences*, which took place in the framework of the expansive project of the *International Encyclopedia of Unified Sciences*, with the terse sentence: "That is our fate." Preceding and preparing this concluding sentence is once again and for the last time the metaphor of the sea journey, now expanded into a parable and carried out to the point of overclarification. The seafarers, whom one now has to think of as representatives of the "Unity of Science" movement, have fallen prey to a bigger task than keeping their ship seaworthy through repairs using things found on board—now a new form is to be given to a hull of roundish heaviness, a form described as "more fish-like." The task no longer concerns sheer self-preservation but rather an optimizing function—it concerns the timely stylishness of a science brought to unified form. The sea seems to be full of material; the end of the Second World War comes to mind, even if the war may have delivered little wood: "In addition to the wood of the old structure, they use driftwood to reshape the skeleton and hull of their ship." Neurath describes the storms and the waves to be braved; the threat posed by the inevitable leak during such a procedure. Still, it is not an entirely open conclusion, when Neurath concludes by saying that a new ship arises step by step from the old one—the seafarers of his earlier days who were satisfied with survival have now become dreamers who "are already thinking of a new structure while they are still building." Piscine form is not yet sufficient for them; but with respect to what comes next, Neurath, a lifelong programmatic thinker, admits that they would "not always be of the same opinion." This doesn't cause them, however, to fail as the Babylonians did with their tower. The rapidity of utopia works with what is completely new and could weaken all differences: "The entire matter will proceed in a way that we cannot even imagine today." And it is precisely this cluelessness about the completely different ship that deserves to be called once again, following Napoleon's formulation, "our fate"—or is condemned to be called it. The utopian risk would perhaps not be so astonishing or even so disturbing, if one had not begun to build it when there was no necessity; it was not a question of a ship that stayed afloat, but rather of one that triumphed over the water. The lack of necessity set free the opinions. And this once again produced an open conclusion.

Something Like a World Order

The Secrecy of All-too-easy Formulas

The idea of a world order, even when it cannot be proven in an ostensible-phenomenal fashion, seems to dwell ineradicably in human consciousness. It has manifested itself in sublime and banal forms. The philosophically attuned soul shies away from all-too-easy formulas— but they are what everything else is based on.

Saying that everything has its price may smack of the cash nexus, but it is the foundation of almost all cults and rituals, down to the abstract interpretation of the core of Christian history as the attainment of infinite satisfaction through the Son of God. This inexhaustible fund already contains *in nuce* the idea of an infinite history whose most horrible debts and errors will be atoned for once and for all, and in advance: for whatever has happened and may still happen.

Where nothing is given, nothing can be taken: Pascal's idea of the wager with a finite ante for infinite winnings as an always justified "game," no matter how slim the chances of winning may be. Conceptualized on the thinking of [the Abbey of] Port-Royal, as an apology for Christianity, and especially for its ascetic aspects, this idea is also ultimately a refined version of a banal conception: in order to cash out, one first has to pay in.

All this would perhaps appear as a base variety of worldly wisdom, as moralistics, as popular philosophy—if philosophy's earliest heights hadn't begun with a formula for cosmological compensation in Anaximander's dictum: "Whence things have their origin, thence also their demise happens, according to necessity; for they pay each other repentance and recompense for their injustice according to the regulations of time."

It can be presumed that we could not live without at least a secret, stolen, denied agreement with this sentence. We are embarrassed to stand by it, because we have the antagonistic wish that life could be tolerated without this "ulterior motive": a life that legitimates itself from itself, a life that does not need a world order.

Here for once faith stands opposed to hope.

Missing Timeliness

All objections to progress could come down to the fact that it hasn't taken us far enough yet.

As soon as it is not a matter of technical-scientific progress but of moral progress, this objection almost goes without saying. Here, however, there is no way out, neither a way back nor a going astray: every shortfall means falling behind. The moral subject—which has to be considered capable of infinite perfection because it is simultaneously under the sway of an absolute claim and finite conditions—can always refer to the fact that it would be easier (though not first and foremost possible) to obey moral law in another world with more favorable conditions, conditions resulting from a progress that has already occurred. Suppositions about cosmic metempsychosis are based on this.

Schopenhauer writes rather bluntly of the belief in a gradual moral ascent to ever-greater perfections: "It's a shame that we didn't start earlier: we would already be there."

If those who think that their own involvement was all that was lacking for the world to be what it should be are correct, their contemporaries were cruelly condemned to be born a bit too early for the improved world. The actuality of the present is annoying insofar as it is almost no longer necessary. Since we cannot bear this thought hovering over ourselves and our only life, the logical conclusion will not be drawn.

A Talent for Guilt

There is an aptitude for feeling guilty. Raymond Aron reports in his memoirs that he felt guilty even as a child, and continued to do so almost his whole life. Of what? For what? One can't help thinking that with this gift, the contents, causes, and states of indebtedness arrive entirely on their own and as if ordered.

Should one call it a fateful life talent? If one listened to the guilty, one would have to do so. It looks as if they are in need of redemption. And are alone in this.

On the other hand, those who have an aptitude for innocence—or, more precisely, lack all talent for guilt—are scarcely more gratifying. Never and not for anything do they bear their share or even admit it; they are incapable of doing so. Sunny souls, they pass over their smaller and bigger breaches of promise, trust, and identity, and their forgetfulness, with an unclouded expression. This, however, doesn't make their potential victims happy.

Here the little Aron is already more consolatory. He never gets over bearing a tiny bit of the guilt for the failure of his father, whom one should have advised to sell his stocks in time before they became utterly worthless. A role in life was thus imposed on the son: to take revenge for his father's fate—revenge on fate itself. When Aron is appointed professor at the Collège de France and receives an honorary doctorate in Jerusalem, he realizes, and says, that his guilt for his father has been paid off. *Fatum* has lost.

What is oppressive [*das Bedrückende*] about the two aptitudes is not a matter of the quality or its opposite. What is oppressive is that such a life-difference is even allowed to be a matter of talent and natural gift at all. One therefore most easily forgives those who resolutely deny such talent. Or are they among those who lack the talent for guilt? Among those who don't know what is being talked about?

Visibility

In 1930, a budding philosopher writes in his postdoctoral thesis: "Perhaps no one has correctly understood what I want, unless one sees that the visibility of things is actually to be experienced only against the backdrop of absolute negativity."

It may be that in the year 1930, one couldn't expect readers to understand this. A half a century later, anyone who has even fleetingly glimpsed the sights the earth offers from outer space gets the point. For its inhabitants, the earth was always the last word in invisibility. It was beneath one's feet, self-evident and unobtrusive, not before one's eyes. What was missing was precisely negation as the prerequisite of conspicuousness.

The view from outer space reveals the earth—so to speak—in a sea of negativity: an island in the nothingness. This makes it eminently visible: painfully clear.

Detours

Only by taking detours can we exist. If everyone took the shortest route, only one person would arrive.

There are an infinite number of detours from point of departure to destination, but only one shortest way. Culture consists in detours—finding and cultivating them, describing and recommending them, revaluing and bestowing them. Culture therefore seems inadequately rational, because strictly speaking only the shortest route receives reason's seal of approval. Everything right and left along the way is superfluous and can justify its existence only with difficulty. It is, however, the detours that give culture the function of humanizing life. In the strictness of its exclusions, the supposed "art of life" that takes the shortest routes is barbarism.

The full use of the world is only a side benefit of the culture of detours. Indeed, it does not suffice that an act of creation could have produced the world; only then would it contain more than is necessary for merely maintaining being. If the world displays the superfluous, then the world's meaning corresponds to taking the paths of the superfluous: detouring all the way through it.

If detours are taken, not everyone experiences everything. But in exchange, everyone doesn't experience the same thing, as would be the case when taking the shortest route. The other way around: if letting everyone take detours succeeds, everything has the prospect of being experienced. The world gains meaning through the detours of culture in it. Or, expressed somewhat more reverently, the world receives confirmation of its meaning in the same way that the many receive confirmation that they are not just a few or, worse still, only one.

It is detours that lend intersubjectivity its significance beyond the constitution of theoretical objectivity. In principle, everyone has something *in pectore* [in the breast] for everyone else, which only he can give away and which allows him to lay claim to what the other person, for his part, has taken *ad notam* [notice of] along the way. For what other reason, beyond all theoretical objectifications, are only the unique aspects of individuals worth knowing for us? In addition to memoirs and biographies, even the invented lives in epic literature are, from a topographical perspective, utilizations of factually unutilized or as such undescribed detours.

In this system for mitigating barbarism called culture, there are naturally also disadvantages. They consist in every path as a detour being the result of an "opinion" or of an affinity to such an opinion. The irreconcilability of the pluralism of worldviews is a risk, but a sufficiently reasonable one.

King Pyrrhus · Life as a Detour

Montaigne relates [in "De l'inequalité qui est entre nous," chap. 42 of the *Essais*] what has been transmitted about the ancient King Pyrrhus [of Epirus, 319–272 BCE], the inventor of the pyrrhic victories that have so often been won. In Montaigne's telling, Pyrrhus proposed to start by conquering Italy; then Gaul and Spain; and finally Africa. Before these ventures, the king revealed his plans to his advisor Cyneas and was asked in return what he wanted to do when there was nothing left to conquer. The king replied that he would then retire and enjoy his life.

At first glance, the wise advisor Cyneas's objection is highly plausible: Why doesn't he just do right away what he plans on doing at the end of such great ambitions? Montaigne reports this wisdom as if it were simply irrefutable and compelling, applicable to all comparably greater and lesser plans in history.

The advice of taking the shortest path between plan and goal, intention and fulfillment has the appearance of rationality on its side. The extreme case of conquering the world seems to be a useless detour, a foolish way to attain with the greatest of difficulties something that a king could have more easily than all others without this effort. A king perhaps wouldn't even need to raise taxes in order to retire.

But do Cyneas's wise advice and the skeptical Montaigne's agreement so much later have anything to do with insight into the human heart and human nature? Can one retire without first having been sufficiently restless? Can one enjoy a restful retirement without first long enough denying oneself its enjoyment? To have carried the anticipation of retirement around an entire world is the ultimate detour. Without approximating this, there is no reaching the goal of giving up reaching goals.

The other question is political. Can a king retire as long as there is still someone in the world who could disturb him, even if one cannot know whether this person wants to? A king can be disturbed by anyone who has the power to do so. The only way he can eliminate possible disturbers of his retirement is to conquer all of them first. From a political perspective, the world is always a world of possible disturbances. The world only stops being this when the one who doesn't like to be disturbed subjects the entire world.

In this respect, the king's detour over the known earth is also the detour of humanity through nature. It is not so much controlling nature's forces and extracting its materials as rising above nature's ability to disturb humanity in controlling its forces and extracting its materials that allows humanity to step back from its helplessness. Nevertheless, without doing away with death, total mastery of nature would mean nothing. However, if death were eliminated, that mastery would have to be shared with so many that a total politicization of human existence would be the consequence of its completed naturalness [*Naturalität*].

Not even a perfect science would ever be able to make humans immortal in the sense of not being able to be killed in an unnatural way—and here we are all subject to the risk of someone else turning out to be an exponential King Pyrrhus, who will retire only after comprehensively carrying out the greatest of all life plans.

Systematics of Fate

When Dante in his great poem described the divine execution of punishment and reward in the three-storied beyond as a correspondence of surprising diversity between the concluded earthly life and the provisional or ultimate accommodation and treatment after this life, he certainly had to use his imagination, given the lack of reliable information, but he scarcely gives the impression of capriciousness otherwise associated with this organ for removing the deficiencies of experience. The principle of strict retribution, of an exact symmetry between action and treatment, deed and judgment, history and fate, allowed Dante's contemporaries and readers to participate with amazement again and again in the imaginary sight of what was appropriate, an appropriateness made evident by the *ius talionis*. This is something like the moral-juridical representative of the archaic explanation of all knowledge: like always only understands like and, therefore, one already has to be what one supposedly has the prospect of grasping. Even Kant—who not incidentally only found the penal principle of strict correspondence to be satisfactory in the philosophy of law—upon closer examination offers merely the last and decisive variant of this seemingly primitive and despised principle of knowledge.

The difficulties in exploring the divine world order get incomparably greater when the trust and interest in executing it in the hereafter wane, and to the same degree, the demand grows louder that one must be able to show and prove part—if not a bit more—of a reasonable systematics of things, people, and histories here and now. Even if the agenda of a "theo-

dicy" refers above all to the quality of creation, to the reasonable propor-
tioning of what is good and what is regrettable in the world, one cannot
fail to include within this complex the role of human actions in the course
of the world and their compensation in it. The systematics of time and history must complete or even replace what in no way satisfies this standard
whenever one gazes at the world.

Theodicy is a part of the larger exertion of thought encompassing modernity. This thought seeks to lead the world toward self-maintenance,
to ascribe to it something like an inner balance that relieves it of external
attacks against protecting its survival and makes it entirely clear to reason
that, on the whole, there are no grounds for the world's demise—even
when Lisbon is reduced to ruins.

Wasn't it precisely on All Saints' Day in 1755 in Lisbon that the Inquisi-
tion staged an orgy of burnings at the stake, an orgy that at the very same
moment disappeared from the face of the earth through a rare flash of divine justice? On such grounds, at any rate, the great systematizer of nature
Linnaeus [Carl von Linné] contended with pleasure that things are no less
orderly in the morality of history than in the classification of plants and
animals, or so he wrote in the private notes he left for the education of his
son entitled *Nemesis divina*. As in the classification of plants and animals,
the correspondence of misdeed and punishment is eidetic and surely not
only quantitative. Therefore, the objection that people had been burned at
the stake in this city on so many previous All Saints' Days without a hint
of divine wrath matters little. What does matter is that on this central day
in the persecution of heretics, half of the earth quaked (*tremente dimidio
orbe*); and the event that everywhere else shook the optimism in the best
of all possible worlds strengthened the worldview of the Swedish lover of
order. He didn't forget to add that God let it be known that He knows the
victims, hears them, and pities them—even the godless ones among them
(*licet athaeorum*). A beautiful thought. It is only amazing that despite his
desire for precision in researching fate, Linnaeus had to leave a gap in the
text: for the year of the destruction of Lisbon. This he had forgotten.

In an individual history, in a biography—the genre Linnaeus employs
for the majority of his confidential statements on world order—the piece
of evidence for an eidetic correspondence must emerge in a more impressive manner than in world history, if the evidence is to result in an immanent *Commedia divina*. With this claim, the person investigating secret
retributions can quickly and all too greatly be hindered by the burden of

proof, if he expects that the same organ that committed the crime must also be the one where the world order proves itself: "Per quod quis peccat per id punitur [That by which one sins is also the means of one's punishment]." To be on the safe side, Linnaeus crossed out this line.

There is still one piercing remnant: the question concerning the reversal of such proofs for a world order. The denser the trail of successive correspondences is or is thought to be, the more threatening the possibility of taking an obvious misfortune and deducing its equivalence in a secret misdeed. This secret unjust act could justify the justice introduced into the course of the world. It gets even worse—one scarcely dares to say it—if a bit of happiness and contentment in one's life leads to the certain conviction that this can or must bear witness to the moral quality of one's life up to now. Therefore, a moment of shocking disillusionment arrives when the reader runs across Linnaeus's last entry: "Thank you, great, omnipotent God, for all the good you have done for me in this world."

In any other text, this line would be a flourish that the reader—depending upon his own pious or impious resoluteness—receives amiably or not so amiably. Only a pedant would take offense or pleasure in it. But after all the carefully registered cases of life-outcomes that oppose this thought, one can hardly keep the necessary distance. Can one use such effort to convince oneself of the reliability of the world order in order to ultimately accept being spared by fate as equal evidence for the orderliness of things?

Perhaps even for this last entry of concluding self-consolation Linnaeus's warning holds: "Cave ne audiat Nemesis [Beware, lest Nemesis be listening]."

A Case of Melancholy

Searching for God's plans for the world, Linnaeus looked for His justice as concealed in individual lives: the symmetry of deed and consequence, guilt and punishment, arrogance and fall. The collection of materials entitled *Nemesis divina* also pursues these traces. Admittedly, one can no longer learn from it how fair and just things secretly are in the world—nor how this justice occasionally even shows itself unexpectedly. At the very most, one can learn where another time *recognized* justice prevailing over fates as a biographically graspable enforcement.

It happened to a professor of Greek at the University of Uppsala, one

Buscagrius, who despite all his erudition got a quotation from one of the classical authors wrong in a dissertation defense. His opponent in the academic exercise pounced on the mistake and disparaged it, as was his responsibility given his position. The exchange of words got fierce and intensified to the point of Buscagrius calling on God to let him never teach again if the passage weren't there in the text just as he had quoted it.

The conclusion has to be related in the laconic manner characterizing this collector of tales of justice: "Comes home, sees that he had wrongly quoted, becomes melancholic, dies two years later. Never teaches again."

At least he is punished neither for falsely quoting nor for overvaluing quoting. He himself had prescribed the penalty for the scholarly mistake, had he made one, which he had thought impossible. This Buscagrius is a King Oedipus whose tragedy consists in having committed no patricide.

The reader of a later age contemptuous of erudition starts to ponder. If rhetorical need still commonly led to such oaths today, no one would teach.

But, no, should the occasion arise, our quoters wouldn't become melancholic.

And no again: they wouldn't even realize that they had quoted wrongly. The quotation was already wrong in the text they quoted.

Border Post and Gravestone · A Daemon's World Orders

What is most astonishing about the history of cosmic speculations is the sense of self-evidence with which absolutely every corner of the universe has been accepted as inhabitable; and this was not even predominantly the case in the century of reason, when it was sufficient to rhetorically present humans (who were anyway concerned about the state of their rationality) with the mere image of higher rational beings, just as one would present the fictive travels of exotic tourists from distant and ancient cultures or from tribes of culturally prehistorical uninhibitedness. Indeed, the eighteenth century held up the thought of a rationally populated world as a way to compare itself with the possibilities of a faculty of reason not limited by adverse circumstances and old burdens. On the other hand, the nineteenth century—now standing under the impression of the cosmogonies of Kant and Laplace—found the same results everywhere from such developments: the occurrence of solar systems in outer space and the emergence of earthlike living conditions in such systems, all viewed as the expression of homogeneous natural lawfulness.

The nineteenth century thought less about the superiority of a few than about the equality of all in the universe.

With Schopenhauer after the middle of the century, the basic idea arose that there could be no development beyond humanity, because any being belonging to a type higher than humanity would endure neither life as it was nor the fact that it couldn't be different. Thus, a higher being would put an end to its life at the earliest perception of its insufferableness. This strained and not even reluctant self-maintenance, one that gave humanity its character, could be thought of as only a bit below the threshold of completely valid rationality.

In the small cosmology that Schopenhauer wrote down in the *Paralipomena*, an organic—if not indeed human—settlement of the solar system's planets constitutes the presupposition of their systematics in such a self-evident way that the little planets (because of the premature exhaustion of their endogenous heat supplies) are closest to the sun in order to be able to take from it what they lack for life, while the big planets (because of their much longer self-sufficiency in heat) can be so much farther from the sun that its rays are scarcely still significant for them.

Violations of this principle of order have to be accepted like other unpleasantnesses in nature. As almost to be expected, the serious violation comes in the form of the many planetoids between Mars and Jupiter. To be sure, the theory of the astronomer [Wilhelm] Olbers offers a comforting justification for these planetoids: they are fragments from a previously solid and integral planet that once satisfied the norms of the principle of order. The assumed catastrophe is, however, no less scandalous regarding the purposiveness of nature than the discovery (one explained by this purposiveness) of a swarm of bodies in space that are much too small from a systematic perspective.

This is the point where Schopenhauer can show his teeth. However, yet again only on the condition that inhabitability *must* be something like the constant property of bodies in the solar system. Thus, in the case of a hypothetically posited catastrophe, some grounds for concern about the fate of the inhabitants would exist. With respect to the planetoids, one can only hope "that the catastrophe occurred before the planet was inhabited."

This meant equating the provident care [*Fürsorge*] of nature with the concern [*Besorgnis*] of its observer. Precisely on the premise of the world being universally inhabited, there is not a lot of room for trust in a philosophical system that altogether denies this world a justification for being, regardless of what concessions in particular may be made to human benevolence on this premise. Therefore, Schopenhauer interrupts himself and puts an end to the expectation of life's conditions undergoing a timely cancellation before their beginning: "We know, however, the ruthlessness of nature:—'I stand for nothing,' it says."

The prevailing sense of life in the universe being self-evident rests not only on the premise of similar results in cosmogony, in the general dispersal of a systematic pattern of suns and planets. It is also based on the advanced knowledge of life's evolution and its stupendous ability to adapt to conditions that deviate widely from its normal, favorable treatment on earth. The latitude of tolerance in the conditions that make life possible is not used up by what occurs in the terrestrial differences between the poles and the equator. Schopenhauer makes fun of a viewpoint that takes this leeway as its standard, calling such thinking "small-town." The conclusion that a lack of atmosphere and water means an absence of life would for Schopenhauer be found under the trusted motto "Partout comme chez nous [Everywhere just like here at home]." Thinking in such a limited manner fails to recognize the essential characteristic of all life—metabolism: "The constant change of material amid the persistence of form."

As a result, Schopenhauer's own philosophy—the metaphysics of the will as the origin of all appearances—brings an element of free variation into the basic idea of a cosmogony that otherwise always has the same results. In its self-understanding, the will is "voluntaristic"; it doesn't subject itself to conditions. Thus, more is possible than what really is. What is known doesn't provide the standard of voluntarism [*Willkür*] at work in the background. If matter as such is nothing but the visibility of will, then an unknown potential for metamorphosis must be entrusted to the will—but again with the more consoling than justifiable limitation that the will "everywhere strives to intensify its appearance from stage to stage."

What, however, does this intensification mean if the will is nothing but this? For this reason, the harmlessness of Schopenhauer's concluding sentence, which yields the license for reanimating the imagination after it has been supported by the homogeneous system-principle, is an understatement. The conflict between constancy and intensification, between the objectionable nature of what is reliable and the rich prospects of what is indeterminate, also concerns materiality precisely as the objectness of the will: "the forms, means, and ways to it can be manifold."

The fragmentation of planets between Mars and Jupiter occupies Schopenhauer for a long time. He oscillates between, on the one hand, his system's obligatory concession of the meaninglessness of what the will as world, so to speak, herds in front of itself—nothing but self-presentations of its mood—and, on the other, the secret suspicion, if not indeed the expectation, that some meaning could and must have slipped into this universe of representation, at least enough meaning to justify talk of the "apparent intentionality in individual fate." What cannot be refused to the individual life, if only to appearances, also has to show its weaker symptoms in the universe, even in its catastrophes. Thus, Schopenhauer once again returns to the swarm of planetoids and sees how conspicuous it is "that the catastrophe befell precisely the middle-most planet and consequently only its fragments still exist." Why is this significant? "This planet was the border post between the four big and the four small planets."

A border post in ruins? With Schopenhauer's metaphorical deliberateness this can only mean: a broken, transgressed, wiped out border between the two regions of planets, whereby the inner ones are entirely dependent on the sun and the outer ones are taken care of by their own heat supply in order to satisfy their requirements as worlds. The will as a world-principle is a dynamic factor to the point of exhaustion and reversal—in the present image: a border-crosser. The reason the will can stop at no border is its shaping of appearance, form, and life. The will doesn't tolerate chaos. Chaos is always only a free field of action for the powers that the will wears as a mask to appear to arrange the world and, thus, to use the mask of the world's order to suggest purposiveness to the observing intellect, a purposiveness whose trustworthiness enables the intellect to hold on to life.

A smashed cosmic border post—this is an unparalleled monument of the imagination for the innermost principle of the world, a principle that is only graspable in absolute metaphors. The world's visible side "is arranged" by this principle—despite such catastrophes or confirmed precisely by them as extreme cases—"with admirable purposiveness for the place of origin and the residence of living beings." Who would want to renounce a metaphysics delivered for the purpose of such statements? Expressed differently: being brought to speech as metaphors, the appearances surpass rhetoric for a never given, scarcely imaginable final authority of the "thing-in-itself." A smashed border post is a marker that things still go on—and it is unclear how far and where to.

In Schopenhauer's joining of metaphysics and evolution, there is, beside the border post, also the gravestone. It is made of granite and, as the lowest and most solid geological stratum, covers the primal world of the battle of the Titans, which incrusted the mass of planet Earth with its fiery eruptions and contractions and gave it its shape. The granite mausoleum of the Titans was not yet the border that had to be crossed toward life and consciousness in order to give the will's objectification the reality of appearance. However, this crossing in time helps one better understand the border in space as an equivalent, a border where the planet—subsequently smashed—must have formerly stood as a border post.

Evolution in time destroys the idea that there was a cosmogonic and geological prehistory of life with the same reality in which the world of appearances presents itself to consciousness up to the point of the one who thought up the metaphysics of the will. For precisely this reason, the will has to take it so far: before there was consciousness, the will did not have an addressee and a receptor (that is, the subject) for its urge to objectify itself, without which there can be no object. But as a result, a border is drawn straight through time.

Before this border was crossed, there was nothing beside a prehistory belatedly produced as an imaginary condition for what came after. If the world is merely the epitome of the representation of consciousness, a mental product of the will's latest self-mirroring, then the prehistory that begins to emerge in the traces and sediment of this world of representation is a diminution of reality to the second degree: an appearance within appearances and only indirectly through them.

Schopenhauer made up a *genius malignus* whose daemonic subtleness [*Hintergründigkeit*] is drastically intensified in comparison to all earlier fictions by the addition of a temporal dimension. Just as the Cartesian daemon gave rise to the suspicion that instead of the world as it now appears there could also be no world or a completely different one, Schopenhauer's potentializing principle of the world also adds what has been. This principle is nothing but what is expressed in a world that is anyway only represented as its historical narrative, as a myth read from relics up to the battle of the Titans: "The geological processes that preceded all life on earth were not present in any consciousness: not in their own, because they have no consciousness; not in another consciousness, because there was none then. Due to a lack of a subject, they had no objective being, that is, they didn't exist at all. Or what then does it mean that they existed?" The answer to this question about the "time" before the rise of consciousness in the skulls of living beings can only be that "everything that we say about it is not true in a proper sense, but rather a type of metaphoric language [*Bildersprache*]."

The border post and the grave marker are, then, metaphors of a most peculiar type: metaphors to the second degree. Without a doubt, the deceptive spirit that startled modernity in such a thorough and fundamental manner assumed within a mere two centuries the aesthetic quality of a metaphoric spirit [*Bildergeistes*]. In search of consolation, the intellect gets involved with this spirit precisely because it has meanwhile grasped that the concept of truth connected to the suspicion of deception is also only based on a few concealed metaphors and cannot substantiate a "higher" claim.

Three Degrees Above Nothingness · On the Symbolism of Theoretical Insults and Consolations

Humans are creatures in need of consolation. Many more and greater exertions fall under the title "consolation" than have ever been covered by it. Both the need and the capacity for consolation are rightfully placed under the protection of a certain bashfulness, like poverty or stupidity. Freud spoke of the "insults [*Kränkungen*]" to humanity made by Copernicus, by Darwin, and by Freud himself. Perhaps the term "insult" is already an excuse; new cases of the need for consolation have in fact arisen. The question is whether these three names serve to grasp approximately the most difficult form of neediness that turns the human into a being in need of consoling: death.

One needs consoling when one loses someone close; capable of consoling are those who make an effort to meet this need. But can one also give comfort when one absolutely needs consoling oneself? No one can be consoled about the fact that he or she must die. All arguments that insinuate a capacity for consolation and comfort for mortality range from bad to ridiculous. One of the old arguments was immortality; a more recent one is the immortality of the species: of the individual in its descendents, through whom the individual enters the species and is absorbed by it. All this already lost its validity when the notion of the finite longevity of the species arose almost simultaneously with the notion of its development. At some point, heat loss would put an end to the boldest prospects of survival, and a quantitative difference of a few millennia or more makes almost no difference in this fundamental question of continued existence.

Freud to the contrary, simply citing Darwin does not identify the full extent of the insult to the human species. Darwin himself would have had no problem with the idea that although the human race is a product of evolution, possibly its end point, this doesn't mean that it must symmetrically pass away in a similar manner, whether by degenerating or evolving along other lines. Evolutionary dead ends—entire classes of living beings that became extinct in the earth's past—have recently been identified.

Only the principle of entropy put an end to all illusions about the front side of evolution, about the future of the human species and its works. No matter how enduring the individual's significance for the species through his descendents' survival could be, at some point the conditions of life on earth and in the whole universe will disappear, and everything will ossify into lifelessness—and oblivion as well. There was no longer anything that could be done forever. Such a universe, like the universe of entropy, was the hardest imposition that could knock the human species out of its self-produced theory regarding the conditions of its being in nature.

It was not astronomy's theory of the solar system, not its theory of the universe's massive expansion and emptiness, not the theory of biological evolution, not the theory of the unconscious and its inability to be ruled by the ego, but astrophysics and the application of the second law of thermodynamics to the whole universe that spelled the destruction of the last shreds of illusion: the production of an absolute need for consolation in the face of what was called "heat death," using a harmless sounding expression of the last century.

It is amazing that the discipline capable of such radicalism in its impositions—and one almost has to say: astrophysics alone—could still produce certain comforts. I don't want to get into its strongest means of consolation, because it contains a measure of speculative undecidability that can be removed neither quickly nor ultimately: the undecidability between the alternatives of an ultimately irreversible expansion of the universe *or* its expansion reaching a point of reversal toward a renewal of its initial condition through implosion. In this the comfort lies only in the possible return of the same, not in the constancy of something present: the reversal of expansion into implosion, the return to the state of highest concentration and selective unity signifies to no lesser extent the annihilation of what exists than the flight of worlds into the darkness of an infinitely extending space, from whose expanses not a single world's light signals would reach another.

Both expansion and implosion are the return of nothingness. Absolute contraction [*Punktualität*] would be equivalent to the final, mutual abandonment of worlds in absolute expansion. The only consolation would be that nothing would emerge from the final state of cosmogony (which is identical with its beginning) except the same thing again. Instead of this—instead of this monstrosity of a comfort that is identical to an imposition—only a "trifling matter" will be discussed. Approximately twenty-five years ago, a discovery was made that is the basis of the entire renewal of cosmology. The possibility of determining an absolute beginning existed—in conjunction with the red shift or Hubble effect—by establishing a three-degree background radiation. The expression "background radiation" has something fascinating about it. The massive empty space (whose excessive weight as a result of being filled with celestial bodies and living beings seems to embody the nuisance of a disparity) is not as black and cold and inconsolable as it could be and appeared to be for a long time. And this means that space is not the black nothingness that can only be faced with the old *Horror vacui*.

Space is filled with a noise, a disturbance of all signals and pieces of information that run through it from world to world. This is just another way of saying that space isn't as cold as it would have to be if it didn't have a "history." There is a deviation from the most inconsolable probability. The deviation consists in the rather precise three degrees that the temperature of space lies above absolute zero, to the point from which distances are measured according to Lord Kelvin's degree scale. Admittedly, one could object that these three degrees are still cold enough, considering their unbearableness for every type of life and movement. But they are not the most extreme that could be. They are like a symbolic concession to the soul. And, indeed, all comforts belonging to this type follow the line of argument: it is not quite as bad as it could be.

It is not important in this context whether this type of argument satisfies a theory of consolation, of the need for consolation as well as of the capacity to console, all of which aren't content with the confirmation of these states as anthropological properties, but rather want to know something about the "technique" of consolation. On the other hand, recalling the discovery of a cosmic phenomenon that has almost entered everyday language, that is, background radiation, should draw attention to the fact that the determination of the human as the "being in need of consolation" has something to do with its philosophically more demanding definition as an *animal symbolicum*. The minimal heat value that keeps the universe from being absolutely cold—which it never could be according to Nerst's principle of the unattainability of absolute zero—this quasi-comfortableness in the cosmic milieu that in no way approaches the requirements of life puts aside its quantitative lack of value as soon as it takes on symbolic value. This is once again a circumstance that looks *as if* there really were one of those signs in the world and in the heavens that reveals the whole thing to be determined in favor of man—even if only to console him for what was previously done to him by this whole thing or, rather, by the theory of the whole.

The Arbitration of the World

[Joseph] Joubert reproaches the Jansenists for abhorring nature so much that they have to denigrate creation in order to elevate redemption. In Joubert's view, the Jansenists take sides within the divine trinity, siding with the Son against the Father: in this, the oldest of all conflicts, now theologically continued in the divinity, it is deliberately not said that only the love between Father and Son completes the divinity to the breath of the Spirit. The argument between East and West about the *filioque* [and the Son] in the Credo, an argument that split the Church, acquires its conjuring weight after a delay of almost a thousand years.

Something else is disturbing. In no view is the world rich enough to be able to afford only giving without taking. This has been the case ever since Anaximander. The world order is an equation in which nothing can be changed on only one side. That this situation extends and how it extends into the divinity is the painful experience contained in the history of dogma. Already in the New Testament, the most important question about human salvation remains undecided: who will be the judge at the end—the Father or the Son. This cannot be a matter of indifference for believers, since the Son is one of their own, while they are only the Father's creatures.

Christianity was a complete obfuscation of the conflict between Father and Son, between the Father's people and the Son's people. Whoever gave all the glory to grace had to make and find nature to be detestable—and how could one who was certain of grace for himself not seize upon this means of his distinction at the expense of the Creator, who mattered so little?

The conflict in the Trinity's configuration grew in the hands of theology. Theology didn't want it, but also couldn't avoid it. Every one of its dogmatic decisions contains an element of taking sides. One discreetly retreated to the numbering of the Credo's articles, played the first off the second, the second off the first. One couldn't escape it. If one sees it in this light, one avoids the almost irrefutable suspicion that this was humanity's highest game of arbitration and the most extreme of its incessant pleasures in exercising the *superarbitrium* in the world: that things are rightfully given and taken, rightfully taken where given and given where taken.

A Proviso for the Beatified · A Lead-Up to an Auxiliary Thought of Malte Laurids Brigge

John XXII, who resided in Avignon during his pontificate in the first half of the fourteenth century, was a pope marked by an imperial gesture and a dogmatic independence of mind. This is still interesting today, because it offers a piece of evidence for the notion that nothing in history can be so remote and outlandish that it doesn't deliver the trace of a human circumstance, of an emotional burden, of a difficulty in thinking.

Despite his tireless disputes with the empire, the pope still had enough time and spirit to ponder several consequences of classical dogmatism regarding Last Things. He thereby almost entered the history of dogma as a heretic: he didn't want to admit that the souls of the deceased—even the flawless ones worthy of heaven and the ones only in need of a temporary purifying repair—are allowed to reach the full blessedness of seeing God until human history has ended on the Last Day through the Last Judgment and until light is thrown on every last corner. Only then should those who have been exonerated and called to eternal glory reach the final goal of their worthiness, the *visio beatifica.*

The pope's theological scruples had their ultimate origin in the heritage of classical metaphysics, a heritage that the Church had at first adopted in a helpful selection and that then assumed a highpoint in the Middle Ages as an ever more powerful authority. This metaphysics allowed the biblical understanding of the apocalyptic raising of the dead to fall into oblivion: a return to life for those who, through a real and total death, had lost or at least interrupted their existence. It was the Platonic conception of the immortal substance of the soul as possessing a quality no death could rob it of that first compelled the scarcely comprehensible distinction between the continuation of the soul and the resurrection of the body.

Just as Plato's Socrates asserts in the myth of the judgment of the dead, the soul's fate had to be determined immediately after the inevitable death of the body, its temporary and easily dispensable ornament. The theological notion of the *particular* judgment of all the dead, indeterminate until the date of the *universal* judgment, was the unavoidable consequence of this metaphysical condition. Nothing remained then except to hand over the rejected ones without delay to the torments of damnation and lead the chosen just as quickly—or with the delay of Purgatory—to their determined salvation in the next world.

One can easily gauge how complex this solution of theological eschatology was, when one contrasts it with the theological conceptions of the Christian East. In Eastern Orthodox Christianity, the dead are kept in a state of dozing or sleeping until the Last Day, and are thus not affected by the consequences of their lives. Then there is a single day of awakening and reckoning for all.

Now, one can say that all this is so medieval and remote that it could only affect one who has a taste for curiosities. Such carelessness, however, wouldn't do justice to the concerns of Pope John XXII and his resulting deviations from dogmatic consensus. He had good reasons to doubt the simultaneity of ongoing human history with the judgment of souls—a judgment already passed according to contingent fate—since this would be difficult to bear for humans and asking too much of God's benevolence.

If this simultaneity were the case, some would still roam this earthly vale of tears as fearful pilgrims, trembling over their ability to be saved, as the *ecclesia militans* still exposed to all Satan's tricks and the world's pitfalls, while their brethren in the *ecclesia triumphans*—already in complete possession of the heavenly rewards and enjoying the sight of God—could not participate in their as yet undecreed salvational fate owing to their own absolute fulfillment. This absolute differentiation of humanity into rich and poor had to be dogmatically weakened after it could no longer be metaphysically done away with. The solution lay in the introduction of a not yet entirely perfected state of the blessed before the end of earthly time, before the verdict of the divine judge. There had to be a dampening, a limitation, a reservation of the triumphant congregation, and thus a tribute paid to the fighting and suffering congregation.

Here it is not a matter of sophistication. The subtlety of the history of dogma is nothing other than a sign of thinking that wasn't satisfied with the apparatus of prefabricated concepts and premises and wanted to make room for a humaneness that it had lost at this point. It can easily be seen and felt that Pope John XXII's sensitivity here is uncommon in the entire structure of dogma, when one has the disturbing awareness that in Church history there was never any notion of the blessed feeling compassion for the eternally damned.

Even Origen, who found himself unable to believe in eternal damnation, dropped it from eschatology, not because he couldn't conceive of an eternal duality of the blessed and the wretched, but because he found the fundamental premise of Stoic metaphysics concerning the restoration of all things after the earthly conflagration more convincing than the dogmatic singularity of a world history set between Creation and Judgment, with salvational fates being distributed for all eternity. For taking this position, Origen, the greatest theologian of the early Church, was declared a heretic.

The question remains as to whether one must become a specialist in the history of dogma in order to catch sight of such moving deviations and exceptions in general. Perhaps it contributes to the refutation or weakening of this defense when one finds a trace of Pope John of Avignon and his scruples between orthodoxy and humanity in one of the greatest works of German literature of the twentieth century.

In *The Notebooks of Malte Laurids Brigge*, written between 1904 and 1910, Rilke has his non-hero think about the pope in Avignon, about the "small, light, spiritual old man" with his stubborn obstinacy. It was the darkness around him that brought the pope to claim that before the Last Judgment, blessedness could not be complete anywhere, neither here nor there. Brigge adds: "And indeed, how much self-opinionated doggedness is necessary to imagine that while such thick confusion reigns here, somewhere else there are faces already basking in God's light, reposing on angels, and being quenched by the inexhaustible view of Him."

No, for the poet—and Rilke still wanted to be such and would be recognized as one—dogmatic specialization was not a matter of elaborate knowledge. The only dogmatic specialization that fascinates the young Brigge in the figure of the old man is the consideration that the old man himself could not maintain: the honorable inability to obey in just *one* issue the honorability of more than a thousand years.

Unexpected Congruence

When one could first hear the wagging, warning finger on the radio but still couldn't see it on television, it needed a good deal of persuading to clarify its good intentions.

In this way, Thomas Mann was asked by Columbia Broadcasting for a three-minute epilogue to a radio play that was supposed to promote the virtue of tolerance. In December 1945, tolerance had become possible again but hadn't yet properly become reality. The broadcasting corporation's peremptory request reaches the author of *Doctor Faustus* in the midst of the work on the *Apocalipsis* of his composer Adrian Leverkühn, who is involved with the devil in the most palpable way.

On December 11, Thomas Mann receives the copy of what he, in the face of such good intentions, calls "the little Columbia radio play." On the thirteenth, after tea [*Tee*] (which he always willfully spelled *Thee*), he dictates to his wife Katia what he, under the pretense of spontaneity, will say about the "nice, agreeable little piece that we just listened to." He begins with nothing less than a lenient apology for the lack of suspense that has just been imposed upon the listener: "It takes place among nothing but good people, and I assure you as a writer that it is not easy to write a play, even the shortest one, whose plot is carried forward by nothing but good people." He doesn't say how difficult the exact opposite is for him at the moment: describing the dealings and pact with the devil. It is all the easier for him to express his "warm agreement" with the spirit and teaching of the radio play.

Three days later, in the early morning of Sunday the sixteenth, he is in the studio for the rehearsal and recording of *My Brother's Blood.* In his diary, he notes: "Amused by the event." Amused by what? In the recording studio he was presented with a scene that seemed to anticipate what would have to have been the case if the morality play had already been on the coming medium of television. Because: "They all looked just the way they ought to in the piece."

This line possesses its irony for one who, like the author, knew what would be said later, and who takes into consideration that the performers of a radio play about the most beautiful of virtues could have looked like zealots and fanatics. Such people, in turn, are immune to any perception that would teach them that their idols might be false—they know too well what lies behind all appearance.

It is no accident that Thomas Mann succinctly noted his surprise about the physiognomy of the collaborators. In his three-minute text, there is something that relates in a macabre way to this contingent match: a horrible anecdote that perverts an acoustic-optical congruence from Germany after Hitler's seizure of power in 1933, a "wretchedly comical story" that Thomas Mann couldn't help thinking of whenever there was talk of anti-Semitism: "There was this club of blind veterans who decided to immediately exclude the Jews from their ranks out of respect for National Socialist doctrine. Can one imagine anything more grotesque than these people with empty eye-sockets or white, dead pupils calling out from their night into the night of the others: 'Beat it, you Jews!'?"

Shuddering at the lonely evidence of this impression, one understands why Thomas Mann thought it necessary to note that those who were saying something virtuous also looked virtuous. But the conceivable excitement was his alone: no listener to the radio play and to Mann's epilogue could participate in it, and the performers certainly lacked the distance of the newcomer (who only knew the product of his immediate spontaneity) to be able to make this outside observation about one another.

There remains the alarm of the few people who, after the excruciating experience of reading the sixth volume of Mann's diaries, still have the desire and nerve to look at the appendix with the texts in small print (whose penultimate text is Mann's epilogue to the radio play, which Inge Jens tracked down), and who haven't forgotten the sentence from December 16, 1945: "They all looked just the way they ought to in the piece. Friendly impressions."

Missed Encounters

Parable of the Unmissable Missed Encounters

In three lines Schopenhauer relates a story that is supposed to illustrate drastically the solitude of an insightful person surrounded by bewitched people: his watch keeps the correct time in a city whose clock towers all have the wrong time; he alone knows "the true time." The point of the story is expressed in the succinct question: "But what good does it do him?"[1]

The fate of this solitary person is to be pitied. Not only due to the fault of those who follow the public clocks; and not even due to the fault of those who can and do know that this one person has a watch that keeps the true time. They are no more malicious than those who only look to the towers, since in such cases even a little common sense counsels not concerning oneself about a truth held by a solitary person.

Schopenhauer didn't want the story to be read entirely in this manner. The citizens following the double meaning—orienting themselves according to the clocks that don't keep time while also knowing the possessor of the correct time—are suspected of not perceiving an obligation: making sure that the tower clocks are set to the correct time. On the other hand, Schopenhauer doesn't consider the person consciously proud of his watch's correct time. What reason could there be for him to adjust his watch to the time of the majority of clocks? Why should he do this when he has the right time?

The only reason for adjusting his watch would be to not destroy the possibilities for interacting with all the other citizens of the city by coming too early or too late to all appointments and occasions. Ultimately,

---

1. Following standard lexical usage, the title of this chapter, "Verfehlungen," could readily be translated as "Transgressions," "Breaches," "Errors," or even "Lapses." I have decided, however, to translate it as "Missed Encounters"—drawing more on the verbal sense of *verfehlen* (to miss, fail)—since the stories collected and explicated in this fifth chapter circle around failed or incongruent meetings, in which something essential nevertheless takes place between the people involved. There remains a transgressive side to all the encounters explored, but the transgression or breach often resides in the very failure to "click." The title of this first section, on Schopenhauer, "Parabel von den unverfehlbaren Verfehlungen," also plays off the double sense of missing and erring, and could be rendered as "Parable of the Unmistakable Mistakes."—Trans.

he wouldn't need to go to any events, because the peculiarity of his watch would prevent him from taking advantage of their profits and pleasures. Or he could come to the quiet decision to stick to the correct time on his watch but take into account the difference from the public clocks so that he always arrived on time. Here he runs the risk of becoming comical in his own eyes by insisting on a truth that he would have to constantly falsify for the purpose of its utility.

The core of the absurdity doesn't lie with those in the story. It lies with the storyteller. In favor of its illustrative effect, the storyteller assumes that one person could know the true time, while everyone else doesn't. He forgets that the public is one of the determining elements of the concept of time. There is no secret time, there are no secret timekeepers, no individual times, no private clocks. The earth's rotation or the apparent rotation of the heavens predetermines the length of the day, but neither its beginning and end nor its divisions along the way. These are publicly regulated conventions. Only the radius of life realms and life interactions matters in establishing the range that such a convention must have for it to be "definitive" and render all deviations from it nonsensical.

The solitary possessor of the true time in a city with nothing but clock towers with the wrong time is not a wise man but a fool. By disregarding this, the storyteller betrays more about himself than about what he seeks to illustrate: that for those following the wrong time, an appropriate deadline must be set for finally grasping what the one person with a clear head saw immediately. The story is supposed to dissuade one from thinking impatiently that all can and must follow the possessor of truth without delay. In fact, it shows the opposite: why they would never follow him.

In Many Places

On Rhodes

In the last third of the fourth century BCE, the painter Apelles visited Protogenes, his almost equally famous rival, at his home on Rhodes, only to find him absent. What then occurred is reported by Pliny the Elder in the first century CE.

To show that he had been there, Apelles drew a colored line of the greatest fineness (*summae tenuitatis*) on the drawing board sitting on the easel. Upon returning home, Protogenes immediately recognized the one hand capable of such a masterpiece (*tam absolutum opus*). He then drew with another color a still finer line (*tenuiorem lineam*) into Apelles' line and left. When Apelles repeated his visit, his rival was again not there, and he was abashed to see what was on the drawing board; with a third color, he drew a line into both lines so that there was no more room for further refinements—in a double sense: *nullum relinquens amplius subtilitati locum.*

Upon returning home, Protogenes found himself defeated once and for all; he caught up with Apelles, who had hurried away, at the harbor; and with the now sealed friendship, they decided to pass on unaltered to posterity the work made by both hands. The work was admired by all, especially by fellow painters, and finally found an owner who was worthy of its fame: in Caesar's house on the Palatine. When Caesar's house fell victim to a fire in the time of Augustus, the enigmatic work followed the one who had recognized its greatness.

When the Renaissance began collecting artist anecdotes from Antiquity, one was baffled by this meeting of painters on Rhodes and couldn't believe that it supposedly concerned simple straight lines in different colors and fineness. There must have been some object represented that was worthy of the artistic maestro and that provoked a new era of art. Lorenzo Ghiberti transferred the classical scene to the greatest problem confronted in the Renaissance: artistic perspective. The conflict between the two leading painters, Ghiberti thought, concerned a misjudged optical construction.

This interpretation admittedly destroyed the point, which consisted precisely in the notion that the entirety of artistic ability was supposedly readable from an absence of pictoriality, from the purity of functionless individual style. Not, however, by all—only by the one other person who was capable of equal refinement and overrefinement. Like could only be recognized by like; this old principle was also valid for the eye of rivals— and for the genius Caesar. Other people saw almost nothing, as Pliny reports: fleeting lines upon an almost empty surface.

Already at such an early date, an artist's true public proved to be another artist. The modern aesthetics of reception has nothing to say about Caesar.

In Rome

Publius Cornelius Scipio Nasica, [subsequently] Roman consul in the year 138 BCE, had early political ambitions and quickly found out whom one had to approach in order to come to the attention of the public.

This brought him to the home of the poet Quintus Ennius, who had familiarized Rome with the greatness of the Greeks and especially their poetry. In Homeric hexameters, he bequeathed to the Romans the now lost national epic *The Annals*. For posterity, it would be surpassed by *The Aeneid*, which tied the origins of Rome to Troy's downfall and thereby gave them more archaic depth than Ennius ever could have.

When the future Consul Nasica came to seek the poet's favor, Ennius's housemaid opened the door and denied that her master was home. But not in such a convincing way that Nasica couldn't see how things stood with Ennius's presence or absence: "Nasica sensit illam domini iussu dixesse et illum intus esse [Nasica sensed that she said this on her master's orders and that he was actually inside]."

Ennius cannot have been too comfortable with his faked absence, and a short time later he went to Nasica's house and asked for him—and Nasica himself let it be known that he wasn't at home: "exclamat Nasica se domi non esse." Ennius protested: "Isn't that your voice I hear?" That was precisely the point for Nasica: "You are shameless. When I visited you, I even believed your maid when she said you weren't home. And now you don't believe me when I say I am not home? (Ego quum te quaererem, ancillae tuae credidi te domi non esse, tu mihi non credis ipsi?)"

Cicero passes on this complicated story in the second book of *De oratore*. Can one still believe, if one knows? Can one still believe what one knows? Nasica could only have suspected Ennius's maid of falsely denying that her master was at home; he didn't believe her and thus believed that Ennius was at home. But he could only believe it: he had neither seen nor heard Ennius himself. Therefore, upon Ennius's return visit, Nasica wrongly refers to having believed the maid—wrongly, not because he actually hadn't believed her, but because he could *only* have believed or not believed her. Now, with Ennius standing at his door, Nasica pretends and tries to insinuate that Ennius too can either believe or not believe, and that it would be wrong for him to refuse to grant him the same belief demanded by Ennius's maid. But with the return visit, there is nothing to be believed: Ennius recognizes Nasica's voice, and the latter doesn't even try to deny his presence. Revenge thus assumes the subtle rhetoric of paradox.

We are not told whether Ennius felt insulted or how he responded. The story might continue along the same lines, with Nasica once again standing at Ennius's gate and the latter saying that he is indeed home, just not at home for him. With this, however, the story would lapse into sheer malice and would lose the interesting element of wit.

Tradition is kind enough to spare us such things.

In Rome, Somewhat Later

One spring day in Rome in the year 1570, the Croatian-born painter of miniatures Guilio Clovio [1498–1578] visited a colleague who specialized in large canvasses: Domēnikos Theotokopoulos [1541–1614], Titian's greatest student, called El Greco because of his origin. Clovio wanted to take El Greco for a walk through the city in the year's earliest sunshine, which, as he would write in a letter that was not without reproach for his fellow painter, "could make anyone happy."

He was all the more amazed when he entered El Greco's atelier. He describes its state as follows: "The curtains were pulled so tightly together in front of the windows that one could scarcely recognize the objects." The artistic maestro sat upon a chair and was strangely absent: "He wasn't working, nor was he sleeping." He completely rejected the request to follow the visitor to the door. The reason he gave must have been what Clovio settled for: that daylight disturbed his inner light.

Another letter of Giulio Clovio's was discovered in 1865, but it was not at first realized that it refers to the young El Greco, whose name isn't mentioned. It is a letter of recommendation asking Cardinal Alessandro Farnese to put up a painter who has just arrived in Rome in the Palazzo Farnese for a while—evidently, the man had attracted his colleagues' attention with a self-portrait. Carl Justi was the first one to figure out who is meant. Foreshadowing the darkened atelier, a turning away from all the beauty of the world outside, the letter depicts El Greco as having trouble coping with the realities of the capital city of the world, and thus in need of protection at the highest level.

Although the language of an inner light is among the central metaphors of metaphysical Christianity, the expression here can no longer refer to a religious conflict. It is not the light of grace that stands against the light of creation. The inner light, endangered by the outer, is the light of the painter's own world, in contrast to God's outside alien world, who as ever festively illuminates His nature. The troglodyte who has withdrawn into twilight will not and cannot take notice of this outside world. By referring to his inner light, rather than to something like his creative right, or what would later be called "genius" or "creativity," El Greco places himself beyond contradiction, sheltering his expectations from all intrusions. He lays claim only to that which is everyone's due.

The remoteness of this from his own craft, whose devotion to the smallest detail called for the brightest daylight, disconcerted the obliging Clovio. Misjudging the other, he failed at what he had set out to do [*seinen Zweck verfehlt*]—but he accepts this as one of the quirks to be ready for in this milieu.

In Vienna

Upon arriving in Vienna on August 12, 1819, Karl Friedrich Zelter writes to Goethe, the friend of his old age, that his wish to meet Beethoven will not be fulfilled, because no one can tell him where Beethoven has retreated to in the countryside. Therefore, he will not be able to relate this experience to Goethe: "Perhaps it is better that we remain as we were, since it could make me morose to find him morose." Zelter's sensitivity is unsurpassable.

Zelter nevertheless drives out to Mödling to see Beethoven. Along the way on the country road Beethoven happens to be driving in the opposite direction. Both step out of their coaches, hug one another, and Zelter is moved to tears by the misery of Beethoven's deafness preventing all communication. In order to create a more favorable situation for communication, the music publisher Steiner arranges a meeting with both at his place of business in the afternoon.

Still exhausted from the morning excursion, Zelter wakes up too late from his afternoon nap and then completely forgets the appointment. That evening he is at the theater, sees Beethoven from afar, and it hits him "like a peal of thunder through the limbs." They greet one another, but this is not the place to express one's apologies to a person hard of hearing.

The next day Zelter to his amazement receives a letter from Beethoven apologizing for having slept through the arranged rendezvous at Steiner's.

When it comes to forgetting, people have always accepted that no one can avoid being forgotten by someone else, no matter what may be owed. Everyone knows that no one has it in his or her power to remember or to forget. Nevertheless, long before any psychopathology of everyday life, there was the suspicion that even what is unintended might be based upon evaluation and attitude.

Zelter and Beethoven enjoyed the rare good fortune of a mutual forgetting. Part of this luck was that the afternoon's embarrassment couldn't be articulated at the encounter in the theater. Beethoven's letter was—next to the odium of its insufferable and inevitable nature—a courtesy that had to burden Zelter with now being able to communicate even less than before his share in their parity.

Thus, the farewell letter that Zelter wrote Beethoven before leaving Vienna says nothing about this missed encounter [*Verfehlung*]. Instead, he consoles him with another type of balancing out: he knows of the malady that weighs upon him, and not only sympathizes but also suffers from something similar. Zelter can only have meant the gout in his hand; seeking alleviation, he had traveled from Berlin to Baden, near Vienna, to take the waters. His gout caused one finger after another to stiffen and barred him from playing his own music, just as Beethoven's difficulty hearing prevented him from hearing his own music.

Zelter had fulfilled his wish of not experiencing Beethoven's moroseness at close quarters. Nevertheless, through the chance encounter on the country road, his intention was "at least not entirely missed," as he writes in the farewell letter with the biblical tone that was so familiar to him: "for I have seen your face."

In Frankfurt

If behind the world as representation there is the will that one ultimately recognizes as the "Thing in Itself," then all appearance must be "expression," as is the case with the body's immediate experience of itself. The metaphysician of this dogma unavoidably becomes a physiognomist. For him, the transparency first of the body and then of all things is guaranteed to such a general degree that no individual case depends on the demonstrable success of his "skillfulness." Physiognomic evidence doesn't have to turn out to be positive. Usually, it appears in a form that is certain for a particular phenomenon: this phenomenon could not possibly be the adequate expression for an accepted determination or for an already known individuality.

Such negative evidence characterizes the case of Wittgenstein, who with conviction told Frege to his face: "You can't possibly be Frege." More on this soon.

Things like this *had* to happen to Schopenhauer, the physiognomist on a great metaphysical scale. His musical ideal, the epitome of his joys played on the flute, was Rossini. Schopenhauer himself narrates the story of Rossini's visit to Frankfurt after taking the waters at Bad Kissingen in the summer of 1856: Rossini sat a table near him at the Englischen Hof hotel, but Schopenhauer didn't want to make his acquaintance. "I said to the innkeeper: 'That can't possibly be Rossini; that is a fat Frenchman.'"

Schopenhauer must have thought that music so completely expressed everything that can appear of a person that no expressive energy was left for corporeality. In a conversation passed down by the pianist and composer Robert von Hornstein, Schopenhauer further elaborated his aversion to the real Rossini's impossible appearance by saying that musicians in particular often "don't represent what they are [*nicht repräsentieren, was sie sind*]."

This strange phrase is only comprehensible if appearance can be taken as the representation [*Repräsentation*] of something that it [appearance] isn't—musicians excepted. This law of expression connecting the will to representation leads, however, in no way to an extensive familiarity with the world. Such familiarity is prevented by the maliciousness of the will, which, despite its awkwardness in seeking to express itself in representation, doesn't want to reveal itself at all.

Rossini thus proved a rule that determined the exception to the great rule. But to this rule of the exception to a rule there was also an exception among the numerous musicians Schopenhauer knew: Spontini looked just as he, according to all reports, should have done.

In an Alpine Pasture

It is known that on the summit of Monte Sacro at the Lago d'Orta on a summer afternoon in the year 1882 something occurred that was never made known.

What stuck most in the memory of one of the participants was the weather that day, which he henceforth called "Orta weather."

Although "unforgettable" in her memory, it was never entirely clear to her as a participant in the summit meeting whether she had been kissed or not.

Only one thing is certain: the stay on the summit lasted too long for those who had stayed down below at the lake: for Madame General von Salomé, her mother, and for Paul Rée, his friend; he awaited their return with jealousy, she was worried about the propriety of their staying away so long.

The worries of the mother were more reasonable than those of the friend. For what remained in Lou Salomé's memory of this and all other mountain walks with Nietzsche was the language they had spoken with each other: "if someone had listened to us, he would have thought that two devils were conversing." But, of course, it is precisely devils who at all times speak differently and with the greatest precision the language of the time, shifted a few days into the future. What eavesdropper a century later would still have overheard anything offensive?

Ida Overbeck, the wife of Nietzsche's lifelong most faithful friend, reports that Nietzsche was afraid that Lou Salomé might have understood one of his remarks as a marriage proposal: he would have been turned down, since she didn't want this. It is unclear whether this ambiguous remark was made on Monte Sacro. It is only regarded as having occurred.

If what took place on Monte Sacro is to be regarded as less a prelude to a lifelong bond than a diabolical pact between two people who would have liked to be devils, a more harmless scene was not too far removed in time, in which Nietzsche himself had to deal with an unclear proposal made to him. We would know nothing about this if Ernst Jünger hadn't preserved a note based on a letter from Martin von Kattes in his later diaries.

This letter relates the stay of his great aunt Nina Yorck with her daughters Lulu and Margarete in Engadin, where they meet the scarcely forty-year-old Friedrich Nietzsche. Only Lulu, the better-read of the two sisters, knew something about his early work, *The Birth of Tragedy Out of the Spirit of Music*. The result of the encounter with Nietzsche is summed up in a phrase tinged not entirely with respect: "A Saxon with a gaze full of fantasy."

With the philosopher, they climbed up to an alpine pasture, where they all sat on a bench and enjoyed the view of the snowy summit of Piz Bernina.

At one point Nietzsche said: "I could live here forever." Margarete responded: "What, entirely alone?"

Neither the letter writer nor the diarist finds it sufficiently noteworthy to mention that this hovering form of proposal, one that needed no answer, came from the sister who had *not* read Nietzsche. It is therefore not surprising that the one letter in Nietzsche's hand kept in the Yorck family archive was addressed to the other sister.

In Jena

Wittgenstein visits Frege, a fixed star of the first magnitude in his philosopher's heavens next to Russell. Passing through on the way to the Christmas holidays at his parents, Wittgenstein arrives in December 1912 in Jena with a definite image of how the founder of mathematical logic has to look. He rings the doorbell, and a man opens the door; Wittgenstein says he has come to see Professor Frege, and the man responds that he is Professor Frege. "Impossible!" the perplexed Wittgenstein blurts out.

The conversation that followed was overshadowed by this surprise. Wittgenstein later reports that Frege could have done with him whatever he wanted—his own thoughts were so confused.

Here Frege was lucky. It was not easy to find someone whom Wittgenstein would ever say was right. He had the talent (one only pleasant for its possessor) of holding his current insights to be irreversible and final and to pester his conversation partners with the obstinacy bound to such conviction. His experience of things being evident must have been overpowering. The letters that announce the coming *Tractatus* speak the language of philosophical finalism. The world was everything that was the case, and his first work contained everything that was to be said about it.

This trait expresses itself stylistically in the apodictic brevity of his sentences. The nimbus of the *Tractatus Logico-Philosophicus* comes from the rhetoric of barrenness: there is not as much to say about what is ultimate as about what is provisional. When Wittgenstein became a member of Cambridge University's Moral Science Club in 1912, he gave his obligatory lecture on the topic "What is Philosophy?" According to the meeting minutes, the reading lasted only four minutes and was thus the Debate Club's shortest lecture. If one could answer the question precisely enough, there was, well, nothing more to say.

This is part of his sense of things being evident.

Wittgenstein's developed sensorium for the physiognomic fits this as well. The path from the arid abstractions of the *Tractatus* to the conception of family resemblance in concept relations and language patterns passes through the simple metaphorics of physiognomic traits in circumstances and meanings. Perhaps this was something he inherited from his father. After his school gave him its *Consilium abeundi* [advice to leave, i.e., expulsion], the seventeen-year-old Karl Wittgenstein ran off to America; after the usual debut as a waiter, he offered a fitting service to a bar owner who couldn't tell the blacks apart among the guests owing him money. It was the first step on the way to the wealth that the son Ludwig would hate.

The inherited physiognomic sense remained, however, a "problem" for the son: How do I know that something occurring is what was expected to occur? One of the answers betrays the level of "precision" that Wittgenstein was used to: expectation is the hollow form that fulfillment fits into.

This leads back to the situation of Wittgenstein visiting Frege. It would prove to be true that this person couldn't possibly be the one Wittgenstein expected to see. Because Frege would not understand the *Tractatus*. Disappointed, Wittgenstein writes to Russell on October 6, 1919: "I am corresponding with Frege. He doesn't understand a word of my work and I am already completely exhausted from explaining it all the time."

In the East

On a trip to Anatolia in the summer of 1972, Ernst Jünger met a fellow aficionado for subtle forms of hunting, a specialist in moths and hawk moths, who came to catch them in these mountains and on these beaches.

After they had worked together finding the Asian swallowtail and the Smyrna sail moth, Jünger learned a bit about the other man's life story. For several years after the war, he had been in a Russian prison camp where he had begun breeding caterpillars on a gooseberry bush in front of the camp gate. The caterpillars thrived magnificently, and he hoped to see a rare Siberian moth emerge.

When the long awaited march out of the camp finally came, he left through a different gate.

Jünger thinks the anecdote exemplifies not only the fact that nothing can hold back a born entomologist from his passion, but also the futile effort that traverses the life of a collector, and such a life's missed opportunities stick like thorns in one's memory.

This interpretation underestimates the anecdote. Doesn't one have to feel the most devious absurdity directed at oneself, when the sole expectation that had given meaning to the most desolate of days became a deception in such a cheap way? Was the passion's continuation more than defiance versus an opponent who seemed intent on robbing life of its meaning?

The opposite will prove to be correct. There are no experiences that can refute the meaning of life. Against meaning there is only suspicion.

Suspicion comes from a supersaturation in the supply of meaning. For meaning [*Sinn*], there is simply no plural form; only one who had lost his senses [*Sinnen*] could use it. No one who has experienced the intensity of an expectation like the prisoner's lets himself be affected by its unfulfillment. A lack of fulfillment is only distraction from a line whose wavering pursuit would have destroyed him a long time ago.

Summit Talks

Hebbel at Schopenhauer's

A natural analogist through and through.

Siegfried Kracauer on Schopenhauer

"You human!" Schopenhauer scolded his poodle, which was famous all over town, when it committed a certain misdeed. Whether philanthropists or animal rights activists should have intervened remains undetermined, as does the reliability of the anecdote itself. In the century of Darwin, Atma (the poodle's given name) would have let such things pass. For Schopenhauer, it was less a matter of reprimanding the dog than of the public's desire for knowledge regarding a system able to justify such a manner of scolding.

There is something distorted in seeing Schopenhauer as a misanthropist. Rather, he is like that primal cynic [Diogenes] who went about with a lamp during the daytime to check if there were any specimens of the human species at all. This explains how the proof was offered to him: "I've got a real human to present to you a specimen of our featherless two-legged species. See if I'm right. His name is Friedrich Hebbel." With these words at Schopenhauer's house, the Teutonizing *Nibelungen*-reviver Wilhelm Jordan (according to his recollection) claims to have announced his accomplice in resurrecting this national-epic material, as he was passing through Frankfurt on the way from Vienna.

It was something like settling a bet. Schopenhauer, imitating the professional pessimist Diogenes, told Jordan that it was hard to find a real human among these millions of what Socrates called "featherless bipeds." The seemingly exotic Hegelian in Schopenhauer's company had defended the species and had been roughly called on to present an example of that "strange and wonderful animal" to the old man.

So it came about that Jordan baffled the dramatist who hadn't been blessed with humor with the question: "Are you are a human?" This imposition injured Hebbel in the eyes of posterity, because he concealed it in a letter to his wife from May 6, 1857, didn't mention Jordan as the initiator of the visit to Schopenhauer, and claimed that it had been his own idea to call upon this other giant despiser of the world and to take Herr Jordan along, since the latter did not yet personally know the philosopher. Hebbel claims that he would have preferred to go alone. From the dramatist's perspective, if one is Hebbel, one doesn't let oneself be introduced or presented.

What drew Hebbel to Schopenhauer? He didn't need an ally in things human. The odium of the philosopher's inaccessibility provoked him like one of his self-trials. Jordan had warned him again—and thus provoked him again: "Yet I knew too well from my own experience what kind of rabble circulates such rumors in order to deter me. . . ." From his own experience—this means above all that one had built up the wall of deterrence around him as well. Two carefully stylized misanthropes: they enjoyed it and suffered from it equally.

If one follows Hebbel's report, Schopenhauer presented himself as an "extremely jovial old man" who immediately and collegially elucidated to the visitor his role in the world; he compared himself to a person "in the theater who has wandered out of the wings just when the curtain rises; anxiously and ashamed he walks away. . . ." The comedy of his fame has begun—he has no business on stage: "What concern is it of the graybeard's?"

Hebbel believed—what no observer of both men can accept—that they might have become friends if they had lived in the same place. But if this were the case, it would have been his duty as a "herald of posterity"—when Hebbel was born, Schopenhauer had already begun to write—to show Schopenhauer the reverence whose unsurpassable nature at least he himself was convinced of.

Things are different in Jordan's report, where Schopenhauer plays the expert; he had at least read [Hebbel's play] *Maria Magdalena* and recognized a degree of mental affinity: "In a narrow little frame, you give us a miniature image of this messed-up world that is somewhat durably glued together, if only with malice. . . ." Then, however, Hebbel had to take his lumps: the preface to the good play, says Schopenhauer, was bad, almost repulsive. Hebbel wavers between whether he should bask in the praise for his tragedy or let loose his encompassing ire against the slur on his preface (not an incidental accompaniment to the drama). After momentary bewilderment at someone treating him this way, Hebbel opts to be the "dramatic practitioner," recognized as such by the first of the living philosophers.

The brief hesitancy followed by the decisive action gives the visit its character. In his letter to Christine, Hebbel the dramatist omits all mention of his stagey remarks to the philosopher: This day will remain one of the most significant of his life; to experience it he had taken the long detour through Frankfurt so as to "greet the great genius face to face, a genius who may now experience the late but therefore all the more glowing sunrise of his fame." It was not for nothing that he gave Schopenhauer the full picture. He is honored with a version of the parable of the one losing his way on the stage, which Hebbel doesn't want to report in great detail to his Christine, who seems to buy into the proposition that long-time losers have something in common.

Schopenhauer reminds the theatrically experienced poet of one of the occurrences that occasionally takes place to the amusement of the audience: the wick trimmer [*Lampenputzer*] "was not yet entirely finished with lighting the podium lights when the curtain went up." Amid the laughter and applause of the public, "the surprised keeper of enlightenment" then pulls himself together in comic haste and disappears as quickly as possible behind the scenes. Not just any useless person who would have no business there, but rather the bringer of light, the keeper of enlightenment—the allegory of reason itself upon the world stage! "Look," says Schopenhauer reflecting on himself, "in just this way—through accidental lateness—I am still present on the stage for tragic farces, which one calls the world, while the comedy of my fame is being staged."

The credibility of Wilhelm Jordan's report about the encounter in his 1891 collection *Episteln und Vorträge* [Letters and Lectures] came under suspicion when it was compared with Hebbel's letter from Weimar to Christine on March 6, 1857. Things like these used to figure in the public prints; this one in 1893 in the *Frankfurter Zeitung*.

Jordan's recollection has the advantage of making an exact point. The wick trimmer is not a functionless person lost on stage who has to slip away in a panic; rather, he has practiced his light-bringing business and enjoys the effect on the audience of his bit of comic playfullness. Schopenhauer understood himself in this way, while Hebbel seemed to see the tragic mistake of missing one's exit. For us, the conflict concerning the factual version is now irrelevant, because we find the incongruence resulting from a world difference to be more productive. But Jordan defended himself vehemently: he cast doubt on Hebbel's credibility by pointing out that the dramatist had kept quiet to his wife about Schopenhauer's attack on the preface to *Maria Magdalena*. As can be confirmed by the parable's lack of motivation in Hebbel, his version is the weaker one; it lacks Schopenhauer's wit.

Without Hebbel's comment about the late dawn of fame, concealed from Christine, who must have been sick and tired of this lament, the wick trimmer parable would only refer to Schopenhauer's vita. But that is not the case; in mocking late fame, it is also a crude rejection of the poet's claim. Christine would have referred it right away to the self-appointed "herald of posterity," in which guise Hebbel wanted not only to speak for the next generation but also to emphasize his own disparity to the contemporary world. The parable was already a satire on this.

"With his sharp blade" Schopenhauer had rejected "in a manner that was as merciless as it was inhospitably coarse the enthusiastic eulogist expecting thanks." Could Schopenhauer do any differently than to return this cheapest of metaphors regarding lateness—which he recognized not as an event of nature but as a delay of reason—to the equivalent linguistic level of theatrical effect of the protracted wick trimming? Hebbel's offer of a shared late fame seemed to Schopenhauer as if it concerned the "simultaneously late and premature staging of a comedy"—and this meant he found himself "co-denigrated as one of the comedians of fame." Such was the risk involved in merely imputing the intuition of a community of fate to the astute and sharp-witted philosopher.

Had it been like this? Can it have been like this? What makes one distrustful is the banal point that Schopenhauer himself too often called upon the tribunal of posterity to have blamed someone else for seeing in the lateness of fame a fatedness where the philosopher and the poet could meet, both trusting in a posthumous Judgment Day. It was the more generous solution. But both had an easier time seeing at work the malice of resistance against and reluctance towards an imposition adverse to the Zeitgeist. Sigmund Freud would first deliver the pattern for systematizing "resistance" as a variant of reluctant approval, as a variant of verification.

Hebbel had a simple reason that made it difficult for him to trust in posterity for his work and to expect that the future would balance accounts: in his eyes, his wife Christine was the one and only actress who could help the unrealizable demands of his female stage roles achieve veracity. With her imposing volume, she had lent Judith her demonic aura, and trusting her ability to fulfill theatrically overtaxing roles, he had projected onto her Rhodope and Genoveva, Agnes and Mariamne, Brunhilde and Kriemhild—a pandemonium of borderline cases, of border transgressions. Hebbel couldn't write to Christine how the Frankfurt misogynist had twisted "with a satyr's smile" the offer of a late and yet still timely sunrise of fame and turned it into the mischievous pleasure of a wick trimmer who accidentally achieved a dramatic effect.

Hebbel couldn't afford such a failing in life and success; and he certainly could communicate nothing of this to Christine, who already had to deal with life's unavoidable decline. Thus, it was better to defang the parable. Two days later in Weimar, the stage success of *Genoveva* and *Die Nibelungen* began for Hebbel and Christine, which allowed them to forget the Viennese lateness of fame the following year.

If it were plausible that Hebbel concludes the report on the visit with the embittered parable of the wick trimmer and no longer mentions the end of the visit because he had already found a way to formulate it: "Schopenhauer is as coarse and inaccessibly disreputable as I am"—if this were plausible, then it still remains unexplained why Wilhelm Jordan keeps quiet about how it ended, about what the two still had to say to each other. Yet one should remember: Jordan had given his word that he would supply a piece of evidence against misanthropy. Obviously (at least one is compelled to deduce), the Napoleonic "Voilà un homme!"—the retiring Goethe's obituary—didn't materialize this time. Otherwise, we would have certainly heard about it. Jordan had lost. Every word about the end of the visit would have conveyed this.

Hebbel also lost. He had reacted with speechlessness to the philosopher reproaching his "agenda" for "bourgeois tragedy" and had given the wrong cue to confirm the parity of self-confidence. Jordan writes: "Didn't Schopenhauer's fierce attack cause this poet, who was too easily irritated, to lose his composure to the point of speechlessness?" His report, however, only reveals that it was Hebbel "still not having entirely overcome his disconcertedness" that caused the expression of admiration to fail him. He couldn't parry the parable of the wick trimmer, which replaces the conjured sunrise with the theater lights that are more appropriate for the guest. Otherwise we would know about it.

From this point on, Hebbel spoke differently than before about his comrade in negating the world. A female admirer of Schopenhauer's had taken a seat next to Hebbel at a soirée and immediately came to the point: "Do you know Schopenhauer personally, Doctor?" Certainly, one couldn't ask many people this; but one wasn't permitted to ask Hebbel this. "Why do you want to know? What does Schopenhauer have to do with this?" The measure of this rudeness is provided by the reluctance to anamnesis.

Hebbel wasn't more forthcoming with information in his circle of faithful followers, although he otherwise was glad to speak about his "audiences" with the great ones of the time. After Hebbel's death, Wilhelm Jordan turned to Emil Kuh, Hebbel's designated biographer, to see if traces of the visit to Schopenhauer's could be found in the posthumous work. With the clarity of the answer in hand, Jordan would defend his report a quarter of a century later. Kuh wrote on September 5, 1866: "Unfortunately, I cannot give you any contribution to that remarkable discussion. Hebbel observed a steadfast silence not only with me, but also, as far as I know, with everyone about his encounter with Schopenhauer." Once during a walk with Hebbel, Kuh seized upon a passing remark concerning the meeting: "When I asked for details, he morosely rejected my request; I had to believe that Schopenhauer behaved with Hebbel in a way that was unpleasant for the proud poet."

Goethe had also gladly kept quiet and was full of secrecy about his meeting with Napoleon. But from all of this, it is clear enough that Goethe kept hidden a high point of his life that elevated his prestige. Hebbel's silence, when all is said and done, must be heard as a symptom of the exact opposite.

Proust and Joyce

Summit meetings will retain their nimbus even if they often produce nothing. A form of superstition is connected to the highest authority: from such authority, it must be possible to make arrangements both against calamity and for salvation, precautions that no one else could imagine or even take responsibility for.

In sports such a meeting is called a top match [*Spitzenbegegnung*] and is thereby more starkly personalized. Those who compete here for priority are already top people beforehand; summits are not those who meet but rather are the place of political topography that top people designate through their meeting and, if it goes well, their meeting distinguishes the place.

If one imagines that the two greatest novelists of the twentieth century, Proust and Joyce, could have met somewhere some time, then the dramatic accent for the scene would already be set by the fact that each wanted to be the author of a "last" novel and to a certain extent was (only Thomas Mann still wanted to participate in the competition of having offered the last of the genre). What significant words they would have to say to each other, indeed, hurl at each other. Unimaginable!

But they *did* meet. The summit meeting, the top match took place. Everything would be good if no one else had participated—the two alone would have more discretely safeguarded the unsaid than politicians will ever be able to. If we knew nothing but the naked fact of the encounter, fantasy would still have all the possible leeway for imagining what must have been said, regardless of what was actually said. A magnificent uncertainty.

Unfortunately, there is an indirect witness.[2] Joyce entrusted him with how it all happened when he and Proust met at a literary dinner [on May 18, 1922, at the Majestic Hotel in Paris] and were introduced. In this situation, something had to be said, and something was said. Proust asked a question, and Joyce answered. Two sentences, if one can believe Arthur Powers's report about what Joyce entrusted to him.

Proust asked: "Do you like to eat truffles?" He certainly did not take any risks; Céleste had made inquiries. Then Joyce answered, also in the simplest way: "Yes, I like to eat them very much." That was all.

Whoever is disappointed and can't enjoy the question about truffles more than truffles themselves should consider how high literary summit meetings went in other cases—or how they didn't even take place at all. The two greatest German-language postclassical dramatists, Grillparzer and Hebbel, could have met at any time in Vienna for years. But Grillparzer avoided every opportunity; he feared Hebbel would turn the conversation to God and that he would then have too little to say. Each of them had said significant things about God—for and against—and had said such things on stage. But does this qualify as a "summit conversation"? Not at all. Grillparzer knew that what he had to fear most was the banality if the conversation depended on discussing God—banality on both sides. Just as things are at summits.

---

2. There was, in fact, more than one witness. See Richard Davenport-Hines, *A Night at the Majestic: Proust and the Great Modernist Dinner Party of 1922* (London: Faber & Faber, 2006).—Trans.

Viewed from a loftier perspective, Proust's ascertaining of a common inclination for truffles is the delicate avoidance of reciprocal claims to being unusual: unity in such an exquisite point spares all others.

While one can get over the disappointment about the neglected exchange of meaningful things between Joyce and Proust by admiring the sophistication of its avoidance, one still has to consider the reliability of the information. The third person who preserved the words for posterity awakens little doubt. But Joyce, who communicated here the undeveloped embryo of a stichomythy, is not free from the suspicion of having produced a malicious overexaggeration: without a doubt, Proust would have had to confront him in just this way to be exactly the sort of person Joyce didn't like. One catches oneself committing a historical-philological mortal sin when one wishes that Joyce made the whole thing up so as to characterize Proust in one sentence that he could respond to in the most indifferent way possible.

Here one finds a convergence with political summit meetings: their swearing to private conversations and confidentiality opens the door to fiction—but with the peculiar result that it is almost unimportant if "indiscretions" are only supposed or genuine. We expect from each person that he said what he had to say, even if he accidentally forgot to say it.

Dasein's Care

The Narcissism of Care:
The Creature of a Fleeting Reflection

One of Hyginus's fables has grown beyond all possible notoriety in its genre by being taken up in Heidegger's *Being and Time*. Meanwhile, we know that Heidegger read it aloud to his audience in 1925 during the summer semester in Marburg. Through this fable, the analysis of Dasein connects to Goethe's *Faust*. Heidegger had read Konrad Burdach's essay "Faust und die Sorge" [Faust and Care], which appeared in 1923 as the lead article in the first issue of Erich Rothacker's *Deutsche Vierteljahrsschrift für Literaturwissenschaft und Geistesgeschichte* [German Quarterly for Literary Studies and Intellectual History]. In it Burdach proved that Goethe had taken the figure of Care from Herder's adaptation of Hyginus's "Cura" fable in the poem "Das Kind der Sorge" [The Child of Care]. This fundamental concept for the determination of the "original structural whole" of Dasein is thus not so thoroughly theological as Heidegger's reference to Augustine makes it seem.[1]

The fable turns Care into an allegorical figure and lets her, as she crosses a river, catch sight of some clay and take a piece of it in order to shape it. While Care ponders what she has just formed, Jupiter arrives. Care asks him to lend her clay shape spirit, and Jupiter does so right away. Then Care wants to give her work her own name; Jupiter forbids this and insists that his name must be given to it. While the two are still fighting, Tellus, Earth, rises up and demands that what she provided for with her own body be given her name. They all decide to take Saturn as arbitrator, and he equitably renders judgment:

> You, Jupiter, because you have given the spirit, should get it back upon death;
> you, Tellus, because you have given the body, should receive again the body;

Care, however, because she first thought of this shape, should possess it as long as it lives. But since the fight now concerns the name, it should be called "homo," because it has been made from "humus."

Whoever has looked around a bit, if only in the antechambers of contemporary philosophy, knows the profound recovery of Dasein's self-understanding performed by Heidegger through the allegory of Care. Therefore, it is all the more surprising that no one pays any attention to Hyginus's fable anymore, or, on the contrary, the excessive weight of the great interpretation has hindered attaching further significance to what has been interpreted.

The fable, however, makes it worthwhile to patiently wait out the irritation it causes when one engages it and doesn't accept the evidence that it radiates at first glance.

Care crosses a river. As the fable has it: in order to come upon the piece of clay from which something can be formed. Where does the shape come from that lets Care ponder what it is? Is it only playful experimentation followed by a capricious outcome and a belated sanctioning through Jupiter's gift of spirit?

Something is not right in the course of the fable, and not only something provisional. Rather, it looks as if the core element were cut out, the element that could explain how Care arrives at precisely this shape. What is missing is connected to the appearance of arbitrariness that disturbs the fact that Care crosses the river—when she, in order to come across clay, could just as well walk along the river. It doesn't seem as if this were insignificant to the story.

This lacuna in the center of the fable makes it clear to me that the fable concerns a Gnostic myth. And precisely what provides the peripeteia for the majority of Gnostic myths is eradicated from the fable: Cura crosses the river so that she can see herself mirrored in the river.

Mirrorings belong to the Gnostic founding myth. They replace the Platonic element in which the demiurge looks to the Ideas and is moved by them to make a world while also learning how it must be made. In the Gnostic mythologem, the highest hypostasis, such as Sophia, views itself in a mirror. One has to imagine that it is her pleasure in herself, indeed, a bit of vanity that brings her to produce something like herself and, in this way, to put the entire disastrous process of duplications in motion.

This core element is missing in the fable of Cura, and thus the ability to understand her behavior: her mirror image, having emerged on the surface of the river and been immediately projected onto the mass of clay on the riverbed, contains without any further explanation something like the instructions for the artistic urge. It is the same craving as that of the biblical creator of humanity, who produced beings out of clay in His image and likeness.

If the fable's poet left out mirroring as the reason why Cura crosses the river, then it was perhaps because one could no longer use the motif of vanity for an allegory of Care, who has to be imagined as morose rather than all-too-beautiful. But also perhaps because the poet wanted his lowly heroine to assume the place of Prometheus, who was familiar to all the readers and had also formed humans out of clay from time immemorial. As a Titan he didn't need a model to work from. Care needed one—that was certainly narrated not without a diminishing ulterior intent for the origin of humans.

Therefore, Care may possess the human for its entire life, not, as in Saturn's judgment, because she invented humanity, but rather because the human was made in her image and likeness, and thus partakes in her being. By cutting out the heart of the myth, Hyginus removed the clear guideline for Saturn's judgment. He did it above all with respect to Jupiter's part, which can scarcely be called an inessential ingredient in the *Gesamtkunstwerk*.

The Fundamental Concern of Being

Perhaps no one has ever shuddered, as if before a yawning abyss, on being asked or asking themselves whether the world in which we live, experience, and gain knowledge really exists. It was in a context of aggravated self-assertion, which basically produced this one problem only to illustrate its radicalization, that this question was actually and unavoidably posed historically, and thereafter would not disappear. For this reason, the problem's superficial solution may have ceased to be linked to these conditions. In opposition to many opinions that want to view this question as the core of modern philosophy, it must be insisted that none of the imaginable answers to it had any consequences. In each case, everything remained the same. Indifference in the face of what looks to be such a hard problematic already sees that nothing will come of it, because nothing can come of it.

Shedding this burdensome problem might perhaps lead to a search for comparable elementary questions that, whether to their advantage or disadvantage, stand out by reason of their possible indifference to it. These questions give those who pose them to themselves, or expose themselves to them, no peace. And it was precisely this that must have been missing in the question concerning the reality of the world: right after it is asked, it leaves us in peace.

Whenever one can say that Homer has already said or asked something, one can scarcely refute the suspicion that it concerns the ancient stock of human pondering and thinking. The young Telemachus, Odysseus's son, searches for his missing father and yet is conscious that the final reason for his privation and investigation can never be certain beyond a doubt, and he simply shares this uncertainty with everyone independent of testimony and entreaty: "My mother certainly says I am his son; I know not surely. Who has known his own engendering?"[2]

There is no doubt about the mother. Here the chain of witnesses and evidence is unbroken, even without having recourse to the legendary strength of nature that asserts itself in this relation. For the father, however, only the mother vouches. It is her secret and entirely her particular right to conceal what could cast doubt on the knowledge of paternity that the son wants to stake a claim to. One lives with this uncertainty, and the hard compulsions of the cultural familial orderings contribute more to this than they remedy it.

In his copy of the *Odyssey*, Beethoven marked the words of Telemachus for himself. If one can believe the research about his relation to Josephine Brunswick, Beethoven was thinking less about his status as son than about the possibility of a paternity kept silent to him. And that is the other disquieting thought going through the minds of the male members of humanity: the uncertainty as to whether one is a father—in general and in the given case. Hence fathers' anxious scouting for the first signs of a resemblance in those presented to them as the fruit of their loins; hence the pride—not otherwise comprehensible on grounds of beauty— in others' obligingness in invariably conceding that the tangible proof is "the spitting image of its father." He needs it.

---

2. *Odyssey* 1.215–16, trans. Robert Fitzgerald.

It's a matter of the fundamental concerns of Being [*Seinsgrundsorgen*]. Not, however, a matter of the very big and distant question about the ground of the world and its reliability as phenomenal reality. Rather, it is a matter of the nearest and more pressing question about the ground of Dasein and its reliability for what one is and becomes, and what no exertion and no fate can take away from it or replace.

Kant didn't replace the age-old ethics of the duties of children toward their parents but surpassed it with the duty of parents toward their children to reconcile them with the fact of their unasked for and unwanted existence in a world that is only rarely favorable to them. He didn't speak about the higher duty that first supports and enables this duty; namely, that parents owe their children if not absolute certainty, which is impossible, then the greatest possible degree of certainty about their origin and thus of their natural provision.

Because humanity can do nothing to reconstruct the ground of Being into the quality of sufficient reason desired by Leibniz, nature endowed it with an almost unbelievable capacity for deploying all its moral credibility to assuage any doubts its offspring might have about their origins. Anyone who has a mind to destabilize and confuse the relations of authorship among humans should consider how arousing doubts about the ground of Being may cumulatively destroy it in the long run.

Concern for a Final Unmistakability

The technical means of simulation approach perfection at the point where reality could be relinquished.

If written and spoken mistakes are not accidents, then the woman working for the largest German research organization in the 1960s was prescient when she wrote into the data of one of the large projects that, among other things, a "world simulator" [*Weltsimulator*] was required for the project's execution. One scarcely flinched. And yet only the small matter of an outer space simulator [*Weltraumsimulator*] was meant.

Descartes would never have dreamed of this when he dreamt. He appeared to have founded the modern age, and set it going, when he thought up the doubt of all doubts: a spirit who was equally malicious and powerful, a deceptive god, as Descartes didn't shy away from saying, could have led the human race, with all of its certainties about a knowable world existing independently of our sensations and experiences, fundamentally into error and held humans there. Obviously, Descartes would not have risked this doubt, at least not expressed it, if he didn't believe he was in possession of a means to banish it from the world once and for all. That couldn't succeed, and thus modernity took its course: with the half-certainty of being able to attain everything through knowledge, and with the half-uncertainty of falling prey to the great deception in the end. Even when Nietzsche decided to let this pass as the lesser evil and to designate it as aesthetic pleasure, the *Gesamtkunstwerk* was thus legitimized, but the doubt persisted in its intervals.

If one asks oneself whether another century full of triumphs of world domination has sufficed to prove that no error can hide in the underground of our knowledge, then one runs up against the grotesque side of astronautics. One has to keep in mind how often the word "simulation" appeared in the many reports about the preparation for space flights. All the planning's reliability, all the crews' vital peace of mind, rested upon the fact that almost everything could be tested in simulations. In this way, getting used to any expenditure for any type of pretense begins to fatefully cloud one's sense of reality through technical wish fulfillments.

What is lacking is the distinguishability of expenditure: reality is difficult, but staging it is easy. Everyone knows that an event organizer wouldn't mind spending a bit of money on this effect. No less than for other things that are held in reserve in the depths of the sea or concrete ducts—as something not even presentable in parades, as something whose effect already possesses an unknown degree of reality. Now one only shows symbols. Why shouldn't one think of impressing the world with simulations?

It is not a matter of letting the doubters and the grumblers of the day shine. It concerns tendencies whose convergence point seems to lie in a not all too distant future, where reality's compression ratio loosens and dissolves, because the new *genius malignus* achieves the same by human hand. It is not a matter of predicting that someone will ultimately fill this vacant position and stage the now uninterrupted *Gesamtkunstwerk* called "reality." Rather the reverse: the view of reality suffers from the observer's ulterior motive—the thought that reality's necessary pushing and shoving, noise and torment is too big to *not* think about its replacement.

Before anyone had gathered rocks from the moon, I had the chance on a whim to ask a potential researcher of moon rocks whether he, when the day came, could be certain that the sample in the test tube in front of him on the laboratory table hadn't been gathered from some remote place on earth. His answer was that we might find something in the samples that could not exist on earth, but that aside from this, we have no reliable criteria as to how moon rocks can be clearly differentiated from any earth rock. If it could not be differentiated, he continued, we would only have a theoretical triumph if the path of the sample from the moon's surface to the laboratory table could be validated beyond question. The rock would had to have left a trail. But why should we be so mistrustful?

Perhaps only because the *Dieu trompeur* whom Descartes put in the world will always have a little place within the concatenations of our supply of reality?

Concern for the Worthiness of Being

Losing one's dignity, title, honor, or rank [*Würden*] has gone out of fashion. In Germany, the prisoner no longer loses his civil rights, the strayed academic no longer loses his doctor's title, the enemy of the state maintains what was once called "worthiness to serve." But what is truly horrible, the limit-value in the loss of worthiness or dignity, takes one by surprise just a few decades after being written down: the "unworthiness of being" [*Seinsunwürdigkeit*] that Max Scheler invented right before the First World War.

Can one become unworthy of being? It is palpable that one approaches a monstrosity here. Perhaps this becomes clearer in light of the fact that the Christian theological tradition never dared to say that Satan was unworthy of being and, thus, that it would have been justifiable and better if he had never been. This would have meant attributing to the Creator a creature that He had absurdly and unjustifiably provided with being. According to Scheler's treatise "Tod und Fortleben" [Death and Living On], however, the modern type of human has "repressed the clear and luminous idea of death and let the illusion of an infinite progress of life become the immediate fundamental position of his existence." In the modern human's busy-ness lies "the deep consciousness of the unworthiness of being and metaphysical despair." This state expresses itself as a "drive for limitlessly working and acquiring."

For the metaphysician, life's techniques for avoiding death are deeply suspicious. But the insight that death's inevitability augments life's intensity doesn't allow one to conclude that life's constant catching sight of death would first lead life to a ruthlessness toward itself, to a deepening of its undisguised meaning, as was the case in Heidegger's analytics of Dasein, where it became the negative of everydayness: the authenticity of Dasein. But doesn't this belong to the chatter that amazingly produced a philosophy nonsensically called "life philosophy"? When else would death have been experienced so horribly and with such panic than in the century of two world wars and countless small wars that outweigh all the violent deaths in the entire history of humanity?

And all this in the epoch of photography, film, television, the immediate conversion of philosophical chatter into that of the language of daily newspapers, into the professional worries of theologians? It seems to me to be a hollow phrase when Rilke writes to Countess Sizzo: "I accuse all modern religions of having given their believers consolations and palliations for death instead of offering their minds ways for getting along with and understanding death. With death, with its complete, unmasked dreadfulness: this dreadfulness is so monstrous that the circle closes here: this cruelty already leads to the extreme of a gentleness that is so great, so pure, and so completely clear (all consolation is murky!), such as we never expected mildness to be, not even on the sweetest spring day." The age of death dances, an age that could console itself with hopes of the beyond in completely different ways, didn't know death in a more public way than is died in our streets and on our TV screens. When would there have been less consolation, when would one have demanded it less?

It seems that for the life philosopher it is not serious enough that life is destined to die. But isn't this the failure to recognize the fact that life primarily has to do just that, live? The absence of the idea of death would then not be repression but rather an expression of the self-evidence that life doesn't deliver itself over to its negation without resistance. What Epicurus said isn't consolation but the most natural thing in the world: as long as we live, death isn't there, and when it is, we don't live any more. Only the philosopher opts in case of doubt for the syndrome that withstands the criterion of the highest seriousness and doesn't believe the success of what he calls metaphysical carelessness.

This wouldn't be so questionable if the criterion of the highest seriousness weren't also raised to the deciding characteristic for the worthiness of being. But the old choruses that let the singers be surrounded by death in the midst of life didn't make them worthy or worthier of being by associating a bit with the dance of death and getting a taste of the hereafter's uncertainty—otherwise the unbelievable long-running success of the annual Salzburg *Jedermann* (Everyman) play would suffice to commend our tourist industry for the acquisition of worthiness of being.

What Pascal said about the "distraction" of the feeling of life in the face of death during his time, Scheler transfers to the limitless drive to work, to the unparalleled busy-ness of modernity, whose energy, he claims, comes from metaphysical despair. The romanticizer of vital energy overlooks, however, that such a life in the face of death largely corresponds to circumstances where the individual is in disproportionately greater physical danger, compensated for only by increased reproductivity of the species. The notion that a lower life expectancy drives life in the face of death into superfluous modes of behavior and rituals, or that the frequency of a mother's death in childbirth already suggests the regulation of succession among sisters and nieces during pregnancy, is not a matter of a higher worthiness of being. The romanticization or even idealization of this situation is as bad as talk of the unworthiness of being.

Death—which people would have always wanted to avoid (despite the heavenly kingdom) if it had been up to them—has nowhere been seen as a radiant figure of power over life, but rather as a figure of an incomparably greater uncertainty. To constantly think about this uncertainty was for the most part nothing other than a calculation, as is the case with the value placed on numerous children. To maintain that such calculation first began to dominate the modern working person and profit-seeker is simply a failure to recognize other specific forms of calculation, such as signs and deadlines of apocalypses, the quota of Church and Jesuit punishments that could be worked off, and finally the settlement of everything with the infinite treasure trove of mercy found in institutionalized redemption.

And, ultimately, isn't it entirely comprehensible that mania for work seized postmedieval man at the moment he saw the prospect of exclusively determining the quality and possibly even the quantity of his life? Only the certainty of a death through a satiation of life, an exhaustion of life's vital potential, deserved to be idealized. But dying from weakness in the absence of infection or medical catastrophe is relatively rare even today, and perhaps always will be. When he was almost one hundred years old, [Bernard le Bovier de] Fontenelle [1657–1757] thought of death as "a certain difficulty to be." One might easily imagine that Fontenelle, the exemplary centenarian of the early Enlightenment, had never thought about death before this last remark. What superb metaphysical carelessness it would be to believe this!

Concern for Reason

Does reason have to be treated rationally? And, if it must be, could it be treated so?

Strange statements can be collected about reason. As if it has to be applied carefully and with measure, like a substance that requires careful and precise doses, since what otherwise preserves becomes poison. But who or what prescribes this? If there is advice for the use of reason, who gives it?

It would be an authority that first deserved to be called reason.

The strange discourses about reason almost always arise in its defense. Reason doesn't achieve what is entrusted to it; it declines, which it isn't permitted to do as long as it is supposed to be reason, for which however there can be no servitude, if it is ever supposed to be able to promise the end of servitude.

Whoever believes in reason has to be able to excuse it as a believer excuses his god. Above all, because not everyone believes in reason.

The Stoic should recognize that the world and humanity are works of divine care (*divina cura*); especially and above all humanity, which possesses reason and understanding, judgment, circumspection, and insight. But what about the person who doesn't share this admiration? What about the person who can't be a Stoic and can't concur with this view of the world and, over and above it, of the gods? There is only one answer: such a person lacks that which, according to Cicero, he or she should recognize: "is his ipsis rebus mihi videtur carere [This person seems to me to be lacking these qualities themselves]."

But aren't the people who refuse to agree about the world's admirability evidence against such divine care having proceeded truly carefully with the world? In a universe optimized by reason, there shouldn't be people who lack reason. And in a system of reason, the recourse to the unfathomable depths of divine counsel is hereby cut off. What can be, must be. A lack of reason in rational beings is an error that the reason of the world simply cannot commit.

It is now clearly necessary to take the trouble that Kant did to still save everything about reason through the critique of reason. But for this it is necessary to justify the fact that reason must first unfold its own boundlessness and go into the traps of its own dialectics in order to learn about their contradictions and dead ends and finally find its way back to itself.

One easily sees that the very title *Critique of Pure Reason* would not be possible without a view toward a para-theory that in its practiced form can only be called "philosophy of history." Reason saves itself as the final authority by sitting in judgment on itself; and it was not only by chance that this stroke of genius occurred to Kant.

Kant's lack of success lay not only in part but rather above all in the excessive need of the para-theory: in the excuses for reason having gotten into the awkward situation of taking itself to court.

Perhaps philosophers are at a disadvantage in the discourse about reason because of their experiences with reason—and hence because philosophy still has to exist. A sentence from another sphere offers no more consolation: "Even for an advocate of reason, the conviction that one can be rational is not always present. Everything concerning reason remains questionable; the best people only possess it halfway, and it is soon done with." Thus one reads in a 1935 letter from Heinrich Mann to Ludwig Marcuse about the protagonist of his novel *Die Jugend des Königs Henri Quatre* [The Youth of King Henri IV] and the quick decline of the bit of reason he had shown in "improving humanity." Already during their lifetimes, the same contemporaries who thought him "great" had actually gotten fed up with him. How was that possible? No philosophy of history allowed it, for if it did, it wouldn't be one. That everything concerning reason remains questionable is an assertion of total resignation before a court that can never permit resignation. After daring to suggest that one could possess reason only halfway, and that it was soon done with, Heinrich Mann further asserts: "This as a correction, if you thought that I was a man of blind faith."

Was it reason that didn't allow him to be one? If so, we would have in front of us a piece of enlightenment about the Enlightenment.

Taking Care of Happiness

The distinction between a provisional and the definitive morality is an invention of Descartes. At first it seemed to him scarcely problematic that for a part of life one has to leave everything as it is in order to first recognize and create the conditions in which insightful (because correct) behavioral norms could be found and made binding without compulsion. He didn't designate philosophers as regents who alone would have this insight and would then impose it on others. The knowledge that is available to all and thought to be limited should show, as if from itself, the correctness of the rules of acting to their best advantage. Knowledge of nature seemed to Descartes to be the epitome of what would substantiate such correctness.

But this knowledge of nature would also erect the other column of wisdom for the future: medicine for the lengthening and optimizing of organic life. How both of these ultimate goals, morality and medicine, are supposed to mesh has remained vague. The only "bond" between them is in the idea that happiness lies in a secure existence. Descartes seems to have been unable to prove the connection, in which the concept of the *morale définitive* as mere correctness is always challenged by the finitude of life. It does me no good to know what I doubtless have to do, if I am simultaneously all too aware of the temporal limits for reaping the rewards of happiness for my correct actions.

If the portion of life for which a guarantee of happiness is attainable can be further expanded by means of the *morale par provision,* then the chances of the *morale définitive* are bad. The world costs time, and the lack of time is what turns people into despisers of morality. Here one finds the connection between both final goals of the Cartesian idea of method: if the new science turns medicine into a "definitive medicine," then the "definitive morality" is only a by-product.

The moment Descartes seriously began to think about the effect of his treatise on method beyond his lifetime must have made him aware of the problematic that the living could always become the load bearers of the future through the idea of provisional morality—and this, as the unacceptability [*Unzumutbarkeit*] of a dual morality, would destroy its evidentiary nature. This was the gap in the evidence. For a philosopher, there was perhaps a seemingly harmless, because professional, obligation: one person or several people would renounce their share of perfection in favor of many, of all future people. But this schema had a future. It supplied the structure for the idea of progress that turned everyone into the load bearers of history for an indeterminate or even uncertain number of future beneficiaries. Neither classical nor Christian ethics ever considered whether the happiness of contemporaries might or should be surrendered for that of future people. The ideal of historical progress takes this to be self-evident, takes the untested to be acceptable [*zumutbar*]. The *Discourse on Method* changed ethics and turned what is most distant—first of all in time, and only secondarily in space—into what is nearest.

If this is something like the "weak point" in modern morality, then it should be no surprise that the break begins, the doubt commences, precisely with this weak point. It didn't end with the discontent of letting each generation feel that it is in the right only as the forerunner of coming generations, as well as in taking it upon itself to renounce what each generation, in preparing for others, should have no trouble sacrificing. Rebelling against such an instrumentalization is found in the tiny bit of "existentialism" or "life philosophy" that is added to other philosophemes, whatever they may be called, since they otherwise couldn't be implemented. More important is that within the syndrome of progress, and with all the recognition of its obligations—indeed, precisely in their wake—the following reproach appears: obtaining the mere means for a surplus of life possibilities is justified by the pleasure of future generations, a pleasure they cannot have because the means exhaust the possible ends, because the provisional makes what is ultimate impossible.

Science itself, whose idealization produced this entire idea, illustrates the incriminated process: the progress of knowledge doesn't unburden the future from problems but rather increases them as the legacy of the present and its supposed "successes" for the future. The growth of science, of its exertion in work, life achievement, and institutions, as well as in its economic means, is, when closely observed, the fulfillment of the Cartesian ideal according to the structure of context: the achievement of theory encompasses the singularity of lives. However, the notion that science must constantly grow, not only in the yield of its results but also in the effort of its actors, would, from the perspective of its early programmatic thinkers, not be progress but failure. I don't know how many illnesses one would have been able to catalogue at the time of Descartes; at present, the older person looks ridiculous if he holds fast to the number learned decades ago: 40,000 diseases. And at best what will happen is that at some point another zero will have to be added to the number. At the time of Descartes and long thereafter there were—for clear reasons, certainly—no "unexplained" cases, no diagnoses refuted by autopsy. In the meantime, the share of such cases grows constantly—certainly also by refining the means to verify the total stock of the attacking "properties of disease." Medicine has long become more powerful than even prosperous societies can afford. Its potential for growth is incalculable. But the living live with the lives that they elaborately receive and let proliferate at the expense of the future. One day the extended lives will suffocate the living. There is no end. No one could decide about where and how to put a stop to this. Age will become a nightmare if the young rebel against having to bear it.

It won't come to a definitive morality. Even the provisional one won't hold.

If Care Is Objective, Happiness Must Be Subjective

We should be glad that we don't know what happiness is. If we knew, we could be sure that no one would attain it, because everyone would want the same thing. Cain's murder of Abel was already motivated by the suspicion that his brother knew about happiness as a result of God looking with favor on his sacrifice and didn't want to share it.

Because we don't know what happiness is, each person tries in his or her own way to achieve it. This propelled humanity into becoming the species with the most stupendous diversity in its attempts at happiness, with all of their by-products. Only after the fact did one say that one was happy or had never been. No one could ever convince him- or herself of what was true about it. And the truth would never have helped, since the conditions under which it perhaps would have been true were only those of that moment, that hour, those days in Aranjuez that are always over when the piece [Joaquín Rodrigo's *Concierto de Aranjuez*, which seeks to evoke the past] begins to play.

The fact that we don't know what happiness is contains—in addition to the mercifulness of fate in letting us live—the temptation to deal with this problem in a harsher manner: with the prohibition of happiness and with the decree of happiness.

The prohibition of happiness is justified by the rational fear that what isn't forbidden would, when won, let its winner pull out of the association called society, which at least pretends to care for the greatest happiness of the greatest number—and must pretend in order to maintain itself. No one may get prematurely happy so that all can become happy, and so that the happy person, or even the one who only looks happy, doesn't let the others forget what they still have to achieve and what drives them to work on universality. We don't know anything about the efficacy of prohibitions of happiness, because the prohibitions themselves are what prevent anyone who would have transgressed them from saying it. The number of secret forms of happiness withdraws from all determinability.

The decree of happiness assumes the absolutistic appearance of pure philanthropy. It suggests that at least some people know what happiness is, but that they want to "ration" it in order to prevent the collapse that would inevitably ensue if everyone knew what happiness is. This prevention of a happiness-collapse is the implied and rhetorically silenced presupposition of state-planned economies. In the name of everyone else, those who already know test a consequence of their knowledge: they live in exclaves of universality and tint the windows of their limousines so that no one can see whether they are already happy. With the beautiful gradualness of habituating oneself to happiness, they allocate to all a little bit of what they have tested. The fact of people standing in line where distributions take place allows one to conclude that the procedure is a success— but also that deadly onslaughts and rivalries would arise if the supposed knowers of happiness were to increase the portions of their distributions to the extent of their knowledge of the needs of what makes people happy.

Thus all remain happy within measure, because they do not know what happiness is or can let others draw the wise consequences of philanthropy from their knowledge.

Tense World Relations

Heidegger declared care [*Sorge*] to be the essence of Dasein and in this found the key to temporality as the horizon in which Dasein understands Being. Care does not allow Dasein to be absorbed in its own presence; care comes from a tense relation to time that Heidegger calls ek-static. Intentionality as well is called tension and it too possesses a tense relation to time by characterizing precisely the property of consciousness that "never lets" it have its things "entirely and immediately."

Consciousness means that things *must* be waited for and *can* be delayed. In the temporality of care, Dasein observes itself from the outside, from the perspective of temporal positions that are not exactly present. In this, it achieves only the equivalence of its self-externality in space, where it is given to itself as appearance, as visibility through the body seen from the position of possible others, and "carries out" its reality.

What occurs when Dasein's tense relation (whether because of care or intentionality) to time becomes "less tense," collapses as extension, the way self-externality in space can collapse through the absolute identification of the self with the body in pain or desire, pathologically in autism?

The collapse of the tense relation to time can be discerned in the phenomenon of boredom. The self that is cast back or pulled back onto itself doesn't know where to begin with itself. Insofar as it seeks tension-less pleasure, this self wants to be absorbed in its presentness. Thus it loses itself in the temporal relation that snatches it from itself. As paradoxical as it sounds, care unburdens one from busying oneself with oneself. One has to forget for a moment that care is acute self-preservation in terms of tem-poral thematics. Boredom would then be the condition in which nothing at all is acute. Obviously, there is no third term to the alternative of being pressed by the need for self-preservation or, in the freedom from this need, losing the temporal tension. If Dasein's self-maintenance is successful, it finds the center of its concern [*Besorgnis*] to be empty: not only does it not know where to begin with itself, but it also finds nothing where it, in its ek-static concernedness [*Besorgtheit*], had accepted what it was about.

The paradox consists in the fact that Dasein is care and can only discard this at the cost of no longer being what it could care for. Dasein becomes a burden to itself at the moment it crosses over into the condition of being able to become insensitive to itself. At just this juncture the tense temporal relation turns into the tensionlessness of boredom. According to Schopen-hauer: "The life of the great and noble world is really nothing other than a constant, desperate battle against boredom." The names change, and the most reproachful sounding one—no matter whom it's against; and when in doubt, against those who have to answer for Dasein—is the charge of meaninglessness. They are interchangeable labels.

These relativistic sounding sentences are supposed to indicate that the concept of "care" is not compatible with dogmatic interpretation. Indeed, Heidegger wanted to admit theoretical gawping only as a deficient mode of care. But that is a prejudice of his analysis of Dasein and contradicts the analysis's relation to fundamental ontology in the horizon of temporality. Here the approach from care to the temporal structure of Dasein can be reversed. What satisfies the ek-static tenseness of this relation is then and thereby "care" or its equivalent—thus also the intentionality of theoretical consciousness. In the simplest case of the phenomenological paradigm, it can't bear, as it were, the sight of the side of a thing facing it—until the op-posite side, the "backside," is turned toward it. This tense relation between the front and backside is in no way the harmless case of something that can also be different. Rather, it is the tension enacted in focusing on "the thing," a tension in something that can only be "fulfilled" in time. Even if this may be the lesser or the least "care," it nevertheless still is one.

The critical point of theoretical focusing lies in the difference between thing and world, between the inner horizon and the outer horizon in their liminal values. The most extreme degree of tenseness in consciousness as intentionality is its paradoxical relation to the world as "object." The world is thus defined to not be an object. Otherwise, one couldn't say about every object that it essentially has external horizons and the world as the final horizon of its horizons. In the ability to say this—which goes way beyond the difference between the front and backside of a physical body—lies the tension in every object-relation as a temporal relation: at any time any object can potentially be *looked back* at. That is not as trivial as it sounds. It means that "world" always has ready a greater leeway for the kin-aesthetic subject than for "the things" that need "accommodation" (localization).

The spanning [*Verspannung*] of the subject to the intentionality of its objects and their horizons is by all means to be described with the radical element of being-in-the-world introduced by Heidegger, through which Husserl's mundane ego recognizes itself. But is this also valid for the transcendental ego that identifies itself with absolute subjectivity through its absolute self-certainty? Absolute subjectivity cannot be in the world, because the world exists through it. But because it must have the inner consciousness of time essential to subjectivity, absolute subjectivity is unimaginable without tension toward this temporal relation and without the guiding structure of intentionality as the tensional factor of the temporal relation. Absolute subjectivity must have a relation to the world that provides the greatest tension for its relation to time and absolutely excludes the isolated [*punktuell*] contraction to boredom as self-burdening through time.

It can be said that it cannot be said so simply. But when immanent temporality is constitutive of subjectivity in general—and with regard to this last point, the founder of phenomenology and its most prominent deformer are in agreement—then we must be permitted to gather the concepts for what is yielded by this circumstance from our own being conditioned by time and its pathology.

Epicurus thought that the gods are free of care [*frei von Sorge*] because they take no notice of the worlds. A beautiful thought about blissful happiness but a false one. His entire starting assumption was that the sight of any of the infinitely many worlds as they were could only have caused the gods grief and care. All the more so because they were not the creators responsible for these worlds; and it had to be supposed that any glimpse the gods were able to catch would also have to cut to the quick those who weren't responsible.

Yet one must—following the rationality of self-preservation—distinguish between catching sight of a world and being caught up in a world. If the gods are supposed to be considered free of care, it can't be that they end up oppressed by boredom. Epicurus had taken this into account. He let the gods get caught up in endless Greek conversations—this idea at least betrays that Epicurus was aware of the gods' problematic relation to time (despite a god's obligatory turning away from the world, as already espoused by Aristotle) or that it at least played a role in his thinking.

But what should these gods endlessly talk about if not about worlds? Worlds are the epitome of what can be talked about. Husserl, on the other hand, would be entirely correct: it is impossible to speak about the absolute as subjectivity without giving the absolute its adequate object—the unity of the tension of its intentionality. But since this correlation of subject and object is essential, it cannot be comprehended as a creation. This can be learned over and over again from the Trinitarian speculation about the procreation of the Son by the Father, of the intellect by *Memoria*. The connection between what appears to be the eternal "personal needs" of the theological God and what as "world" must be related to the biblical creation is already inaugurated in the Old Testament's logos-speculation that enters into the prologue of the Gospel of John: the eternal "Word" through which the world came into being was supposed to be more than the original metaphor of the imperial command of a city-founder, more than the image of a demiurge's deed. Strictly speaking, it was a matter of grounding God's care for the world: He was supposed to have gotten more deeply involved in and committed Himself to the world than those old metaphors of production and command were able to express. It was supposed to be a "real" care, but this care couldn't press upon the one who was obliged to have it.

Husserl, who took a path too far removed from all theologies and who could hardly be affiliated with a "secularized" scheme of mediation, didn't postulate the necessity of the world for absolute subjectivity in an immediately systematic manner. His transcendental intersubjectivity—as the condition of possibility of an objective "world" for the transcendental subject—is something like a genuine logos-speculation out of the spirit of phenomenology. And insofar as no subject can have an object other than in an intentional "achievement," this primal association is also not "carefree [*sorgenfrei*]."

A Still Unconfirmed Last Word

How does one die in and with philosophies? Socrates would have disapproved of this plural form or left it unexplained. But the question of how one dies with Philosophy would have seemed to him to be the essential question—and the one he needed to answer as soon as possible.

For the Stoics, the question is still valid in the great gesture of death's presence; for Epicurus, it is valid only in certifying death to be unreal. How one died in and with the philosophies that arose after Antiquity is already withheld from us inasmuch as competence in the matter of dying correctly passed to theology and ceased to be a philosophical theme. How a Cartesian died can at best be classified through the facts of its transmission, and one becomes suspicious if it fits too well into the "system."

Now, belated consistency is nothing reprehensible, no matter how much historical criticism may despise it.

Imaginary anecdotes arise here. I would like to know what the next millennium will report about the deaths and "last words" of Heidegger and his followers, and I would not object to a competition that makes suggestions for this tradition.

I would like to learn it from private indiscretion, but I can't. Then the question becomes: what could someone who was struck as much by existential analysis as by the question of the "essence of reason" still have to say at the end? If we had the best possible evidence, what must he have said? Perhaps something like:

"No more reason to worry [Kein Grund mehr zur Sorge]."[3]

---

3. Blumenberg revisits the question of Heidegger's last words in a brief section titled "Ein Dementi [A Disclaimer]" in his posthumously published book *Die Verführbarkeit des Philosophen* [The Philosopher's Susceptibility to Seduction]. Shortly after the appearance of *Die Sorge geht über den Fluß*, he had received a letter from Walter Bröcker saying that there was no need to guess Heidegger's last words, because they had been passed on to Bröcker himself by Heidegger's wife, Elfride. One morning, when the old man was weak but not sick, he had merely said: "I'm going to stay in bed a bit [Ich bleibe noch liegen]" (Blumenberg, *Die Verführbarkeit des Philosophen* [Frankfurt am Main: Suhrkamp, 2000], p. 107).—Trans.

MERIDIAN

Crossing Aesthetics

Bernard Stiegler, *Taking Care of Youth and the Generations*

Ruth Stein, *For Love of the Father: A Psychoanalytic Study of Religious Terrorism*

Giorgio Agamben, *"What is an Apparatus?" and Other Essays*

Rodolphe Gasché, *Europe, or the Infinite Task: A Study of a Philosophical Concept*

Bernard Stiegler, *Technics and Time, 2: Disorientation*

Bernard Stiegler, *Acting Out*

Susan Bernstein, *Housing Problems: Writing and Architecture in Goethe, Walpole, Freud, and Heidegger*

Martin Hägglund, *Radical Atheism: Derrida and the Time of Life*

Cornelia Vismann, *Files: Law and Media Technology*

Jean-Luc Nancy, *Discourse of the Syncope: Logodaedalus*

Carol Jacobs, *Skirting the Ethical: Sophocles, Plato, Hamann, Sebald, Campion*

Cornelius Castoriadis, *Figures of the Thinkable*

Jacques Derrida, *Psyche: Inventions of the Other*, 2 volumes, edited by Peggy Kamuf and Elizabeth Rottenberg

Mark Sanders, *Ambiguities of Witnessing: Literature and Law in the Time of a Truth Commission*

Sarah Kofman, *Selected Writings*, edited by Thomas Albrecht, with Georgia Albert and Elizabeth Rottenberg

Arendt, Hannah, *Reflections on Literature and Culture*, edited by Susannah Young-ah Gottlieb

Alan Bass, *Interpretation and Difference: The Strangeness of Care*

Jacques Derrida, *H.C. for Life, That Is to Say...*

Ernst Bloch, *Traces*

Elizabeth Rottenberg, *Inheriting the Future: Legacies of Kant, Freud, and Flaubert*

David Michael Kleinberg-Levin, *Gestures of Ethical Life*

Jacques Derrida, *On Touching—Jean-Luc Nancy*

Jacques Derrida, *Rogues: Two Essays on Reason*

Peggy Kamuf, *Book of Addresses*

Giorgio Agamben, *The Time That Remains: A Commentary on the Letter to the Romans*

Jean-Luc Nancy, *Multiple Arts: The Muses II*

Alain Badiou, *Handbook of Inaesthetics*

Jacques Derrida, *Eyes of the University: Right to Philosophy 2*

Maurice Blanchot, *Lautréamont and Sade*

Giorgio Agamben, *The Open: Man and Animal*

Jean Genet, *The Declared Enemy*

Shoshana Felman, *Writing and Madness: (Literature/Philosophy/Psychoanalysis)*

Jean Genet, *Fragments of the Artwork*

Shoshana Felman, *The Scandal of the Speaking Body: Don Juan with J. L. Austin, or Seduction in Two Languages*

Peter Szondi, *Celan Studies*

Neil Hertz, *George Eliot's Pulse*

Maurice Blanchot, *The Book to Come*

Susannah Young-ah Gottlieb, *Regions of Sorrow: Anxiety and Messianism in Hannah Arendt and W. H. Auden*

Jacques Derrida, *Without Alibi*, edited by Peggy Kamuf

Cornelius Castoriadis, *On Plato's 'Statesman'*

Jacques Derrida, *Who's Afraid of Philosophy? Right to Philosophy 1*

Peter Szondi, *An Essay on the Tragic*

Peter Fenves, *Arresting Language: From Leibniz to Benjamin*

Jill Robbins, ed. *Is It Righteous to Be? Interviews with Emmanuel Levinas*

Louis Marin, *Of Representation*

J. Hillis Miller, *Speech Acts in Literature*

Maurice Blanchot, *Faux pas*

Jean-Luc Nancy, *Being Singular Plural*

Maurice Blanchot / Jacques Derrida, *The Instant of My Death / Demeure: Fiction and Testimony*

Niklas Luhmann, *Art as a Social System*

Emmanual Levinas, *God, Death, and Time*

Ernst Bloch, *The Spirit of Utopia*

Giorgio Agamben, *Potentialities: Collected Essays in Philosophy*

Ellen S. Burt, *Poetry's Appeal: French Nineteenth-Century Lyric and the Political Space*

Jacques Derrida, *Adieu to Emmanuel Levinas*

Werner Hamacher, *Premises: Essays on Philosophy and Literature from Kant to Celan*

Aris Fioretos, *The Gray Book*

Deborah Esch, *In the Event: Reading Journalism, Reading Theory*

Winfried Menninghaus, *In Praise of Nonsense: Kant and Bluebeard*

Giorgio Agamben, *The Man Without Content*

Giorgio Agamben, *The End of the Poem: Studies in Poetics*

Theodor W. Adorno, *Sound Figures*

Louis Marin, *Sublime Poussin*

Philippe Lacoue-Labarthe, *Poetry as Experience*

Ernst Bloch, *Literary Essays*

Jacques Derrida, *Resistances of Psychoanalysis*

Marc Froment-Meurice, *That Is to Say: Heidegger's Poetics*

Francis Ponge, *Soap*

Philippe Lacoue-Labarthe, *Typography: Mimesis, Philosophy, Politics*

Giorgio Agamben, *Homo Sacer: Sovereign Power and Bare Life*

Emmanuel Levinas, *Of God Who Comes To Mind*

Bernard Stiegler, *Technics and Time, 1: The Fault of Epimetheus*

Werner Hamacher, *pleroma—Reading in Hegel*

Serge Leclaire, *Psychoanalyzing: On the Order of the Unconscious and the Practice of the Letter*

Serge Leclaire, *A Child Is Being Killed: On Primary Narcissism and the Death Drive*

Sigmund Freud, *Writings on Art and Literature*

Cornelius Castoriadis, *World in Fragments: Writings on Politics, Society, Psychoanalysis, and the Imagination*

Thomas Keenan, *Fables of Responsibility: Aberrations and Predicaments in Ethics and Politics*

Emmanuel Levinas, *Proper Names*

Alexander García Düttmann, *At Odds with AIDS: Thinking and Talking About a Virus*

Maurice Blanchot, *Friendship*

Jean-Luc Nancy, *The Muses*

Massimo Cacciari, *Posthumous People: Vienna at the Turning Point*

David E. Wellbery, *The Specular Moment: Goethe's Early Lyric and the Beginnings of Romanticism*

Edmond Jabès, *The Little Book of Unsuspected Subversion*

Hans-Jost Frey, *Studies in Poetic Discourse: Mallarmé, Baudelaire, Rimbaud, Hölderlin*

Pierre Bourdieu, *The Rules of Art: Genesis and Structure of the Literary Field*

Nicolas Abraham, *Rhythms: On the Work, Translation, and Psychoanalysis*

Jacques Derrida, *On the Name*

David Wills, *Prosthesis*

Maurice Blanchot, *The Work of Fire*

Jacques Derrida, *Points . . . : Interviews, 1974–1994*

J. Hillis Miller, *Topographies*

Philippe Lacoue-Labarthe, *Musica Ficta (Figures of Wagner)*

Jacques Derrida, *Aporias*

Emmanuel Levinas, *Outside the Subject*

Jean-François Lyotard, *Lessons on the Analytic of the Sublime*

Peter Fenves, *"Chatter": Language and History in Kierkegaard*

Jean-Luc Nancy, *The Experience of Freedom*

Jean-Joseph Goux, *Oedipus, Philosopher*

Haun Saussy, *The Problem of a Chinese Aesthetic*

Jean-Luc Nancy, *The Birth to Presence*

Printed and bound by CPI Group (UK) Ltd, Croydon, CR0 4YY

13/04/2025

14656449-0003